WEST AFRICAN URBANIZATION

A STUDY OF
VOLUNTARY ASSOCIATIONS IN
SOCIAL CHANGE

BY

KENNETH LITTLE

Professor of Social Anthropology
University of Edinburgh

CAMBRIDGE

AT THE UNIVERSITY PRESS

1965

PUBLISHED BY

THE SYNDICS OF THE CAMBRIDGE UNIVERSITY PRESS

Bentley House, 200 Euston Road, London, N.W. 1
American Branch: 32 East 57th Street, New York, N.Y. 10022
West African Office: P.O. Box 33, Ibadan, Nigeria

CAMBRIDGE UNIVERSITY PRESS

1965

Library of Congress Catalogue Card Number: 65-14349

Printed in Great Britain by
Spottiswoode, Ballantyne and Co. Ltd
London and Colchester

CONTENTS

ACKNOWLEDGEMENTS

My colleagues, Dr Michael Banton and Dr Malcolm Ruel kindly read sections of the preliminary draft of this book, and I am also indebted to Dr D. K. Fiawoo for his permission to quote some passages of his unpublished Edinburgh University Ph.D. thesis, 'The Influence of Contemporary Social Changes on the Magico-Religious Concepts and Organization of the Southern Ewe-speaking People of Ghana'.

I have also to thank Miss Flora Mitchell for the care with which she typed and re-typed successive drafts and checked references.

K. L.

Edinburgh,
November 1964

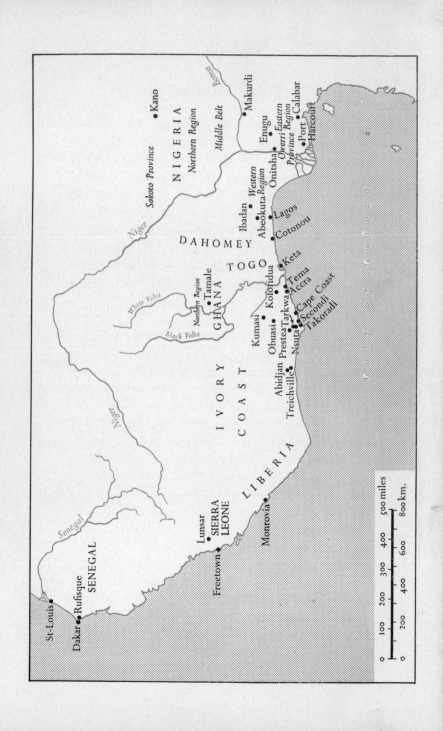

INTRODUCTION

THIS short book is based on the Frazer Lecture that I gave in May 1963 at the invitation of the University of Cambridge. It is concerned with the function of voluntary associations in social change. My aim is to show by means of these organizations that there is a sense in which an evolutionary approach is relevant to anthropological theory. I employ the concepts of 'adaptation' and 'integration' for this purpose and choose a former 'backward' area of the world where industrial growth is now fully under way. Regarding the latter phenomenon as the paramount factor in social change, my argument can be summarized as follows.

The substitution of a market economy for an economy based upon subsistence involves the disturbance of traditional ideas of status. New roles are created whose fulfilment necessitates the interaction of individuals on a basis of common interest in such things as wages, education, religion, and politics rather than genealogical origin and descent. Before, however, the new forms of association can be fully institutionalized there is required a system of relationships which will link the old with the new structure. This is needed because, the gap in terms of social values being very wide, traditional roles have to be adapted and the fresh social institutions integrated within a wider social system than previously prevailed.

My suggestion is that the system of relationships referred to is provided largely by voluntary associations, and I have examined this proposition in the context of West African social change. I endeavour to show that voluntary associations—institutionalized groups in which membership is attained *by joining*—are functionally significant in the roles played in the new 'urban' economy by rural migrants, by the younger men, by

I

women in general, and by the individual with a Western education. Consideration of these roles is based on the assumption that the main determinants of status derive from the industrial system, and so I have also tried to show the relation of voluntary associations to an emerging class structure.

This attempt to examine West African social change as a whole obviously involves working over a wide canvas. It therefore presents certain practical difficulties, not the least of which is my dependence, for the most part, upon other students' work. I have made my own observations of the phenomena concerned in Sierra Leone and to a very much smaller extent in Nigeria, the Gambia and Ghana, but this empirical research has been carried out over the years and it does not add up to a full-length study of voluntary associations. Nor, on the whole, are the available documentary sources rich in information, As my bibliography will indicate, there is no lack of references to these organizations, but as a social institution they have rarely been fully investigated and only in a few cases has any comprehensive attempt been made to analyse their function. The latter are mainly M. P. Banton's *West African City*, 1957; P. Caprasse's 'Leaders africains en milieu urbain', *Centre d'Étude des Problèmes Sociaux Indigenes. Collection de Mémoires*, Volume No. 5, 1959; I. Wallerstein's 'The political role of voluntary associations in Middle Africa' in *Political Groups in Middle Africa* (ed. James S. Coleman and Carl Rosberg); and Pierre Clément's 'Social effects of urbanization in Stanleyville, Belgian Congo' in *Social Implications of Industrialization and Urbanization* (UNESCO), 1956. Unfortunately, the work of Caprasse and Clément, although very relevant to my theme, deals with a country, the Congo, which is sociologically as well as geographically somewhat different from the West African region proper.

An even more difficult problem is the rapidity of change

itself. Not only is the existence of many voluntary associations ephemeral, but one's more general frame of reference tends very quickly to get out of date. This applies particularly to more recent political and economic development. For this reason and because of the scarcity of compact documentation, I have been obliged to 'telescope' a good deal of material, quite often venturing generalizations for which there may be a lack of continuous evidence. The primary objective of this book is then, not to describe voluntary associations as such, still less to write a history, but to provide a model which may be useful to students of social change. What to my mind is important is not the particular incidence of this form of social organization, but the light it throws directly or indirectly upon general problems of transition, including the results of industrial and technological change in 'advanced' as well as in tribal societies. Here, of course, I am concerned entirely with the latter, and for practical purposes this means considering change from the pre-colonial to the colonial situation and as far as Independence. Since, for the greater part, the studies upon which I have drawn were made before African self-government I have not taken my analysis beyond that stage.

In these somewhat historical terms, then, if it can be shown that voluntary associations were functional in certain sociological situations, why was their 'integrating effect' not manifest in other comparable circumstances'? Is it because there was no precedent in the traditional structure for non-kinship forms of association: or is it simply that 'adaptation' was made in some other way? An interesting slant on the latter question is that some peoples, such as the Mende, apparently find it easier to participate in associations formed by other tribes than to adapt to urban purposes their own 'secret' societies. Further—and this opens up a whole new set of hypothetical

3

questions—what is the effect of nationalist policy? Wallerstein, for instance, states that the years immediately following Independence have seen an almost complete 'politization' of voluntary associations in the interests of single-party government. The latter has led to parallel trends towards a single trade union, youth, women's, students' and co-operative structure, in many cases, forming an integral part of the party.[1] In addition, although increased social differentiation coming from economic development might renew pressure in the direction of multiplicity, specificity, and autonomy of voluntary associations (1963, p. 165), economic growth might also be favourable to the welfare state. The latter, by increasing social services, would assume many of the functions upon which in transitional circumstances, the existence of voluntary associations basically depends.

Admittedly, all these questions also require exploration. In the meantime, I have merely endeavoured, by stating the problem in positive terms, to show that a functional analysis of voluntary associations may provide part of the answer.

Finally, since it is part of my thesis that differences in the possession of formal education and of Western ideas and habits are sociologically significant for social change, my references to various categories of person are intended to carry the following fairly specific connotations.

Educated person: one who has completed a course of study at a secondary school, or its equivalent.

Literate person: one who has attended school for a number of years but without completing his education at a secondary school, or its equivalent. (It excludes, for present purposes, a person who is literate only in Arabic.)

[1] In Ghana in 1961, separate membership cards for the trade union, farmers' co-operative and women's movements were abolished, membership in the Convention People's Party offering automatic membership in the linked groups (Wallerstein, 1963, p. 165, f.n.).

4

Semi-literate person: one who has very little or no formal education but can understand or make himself understood in English or French.

Illiterate person: one who has no formal education and who cannot understand or make himself understood in English or French.

African élite (except where more specifically defined): persons in the senior ranks of the Administration, including Ministers, party leaders, and top civil servants; persons in professional occupations, such as doctors, lawyers, university teachers, heads of important secondary schools and of training colleges, holders of important traditional titles; top-ranking Christian clergy.[1]

[1] This categorization corresponds broadly with the Smythe's definition of the 'top-level' élite in Nigeria (cf. Smythe, p. 92).

Part One

I

THE LURE OF THE TOWN

THE so-called wind of change blowing through Africa has disturbed not only the dominance of white settlers, but the continent's entire way of life. A visitor can observe the effects for himself. He will see a majority of Africans living in huts of wattle and daub and of grass, herding cattle and cultivating their farms and plots with home-made implements, pounding their food in mortars, crossing rivers in dug-out canoes, dancing to the music of wooden drums, and worshipping ancient gods and spirits. But he will also find most of the civilized trappings, many of them far from superficial. He can travel on trains and in motor cars and aeroplanes, and stay in ultra-modern hotels. He can visit African houses furnished as in Hampstead and equipped with refrigeration and electricity. He will see Africans working in shops, offices, mines and factories, growing crops for foreign consumption, and leasing and renting land. He will find churches and schools by the hundred and sometimes a university. He can play outdoor games, attend ballroom dances and performances of amateur dramatics, and buy a flag for charity—all these activities being organized by Africans. Above all, to an extent not previously dreamed of, these vast lands are now ruled by Africans, and Africans are developing new and interesting forms of social organization.

There are, however, considerable differences in the extent to which particular peoples and ethnic groups have given up their former habits. Indeed, mostly it occurs that the African individual moving out of the tribal area continues to be influenced by tribal culture.[1] Situations vary all over the continent, but in this chapter I am treating social change in West Africa as a special case because, for contemporary as well as historical reasons, its trend is significant for the rest of Africa.

What this modern transformation of West Africa involves is a process analogous to the changes that resulted in the urbanization of nineteenth-century Western Europe. Western contact with Africa, like the Industrial Revolution in Europe, has stimulated a great movement of people. One of the reasons is increased pressure of population upon land resources because, while technological developments in terms of improved health facilities and child-care have led to a general growth in population, there has not always been an accompanying rise in food production. On the contrary, quite often indigenous methods of cultivation continue to be practised with a shorter and shorter period of fallow. This, by reducing the fertility of the soil, brings about an overall decrease in the margin of subsistence and the density of population which the land can support.

Hunger, therefore, may supply one of the reasons for men and their families seeking a living elsewhere. It probably accounts for a good deal of the seasonal migration referred to on a later page. Thus, of Northern Nigerian migrants studied in Sokoto, nearly all had an economic reason for migration. According to Prothero, 52 per cent of them said that they were seeking money; 16 per cent that they were seeking food; and a further 16 per cent that they were going to trade. Admittedly, respondents' answers are not necessarily the best indication of

[1] Note, in particular, Gluckman's discussion of this point in the context of Central Africa (Gluckman, pp. 55–7).

objective factors. Nevertheless, as Prothero points out, 'the total number of migrants away from the Province for several months of the year must go a considerable way towards conserving supplies in the home areas'. Significantly enough, too, all the destinations, with the exception of French territory, had in common the fact that their economic development was far in advance of that in which the migrants originated. (Prothero, pp. 22–32.)

Migration is also encouraged by the diversification of the economy, because the construction of new roads, railways and public works, the opening of mines, the development of cash crops, and petty trade all offer opportunities of employment. Not only are there a host of occupations and ways of getting a living alternative to the traditional system, but to some extent, as Fortes has pointed out, 'labour, enterprise and skill are now marketable in their own right anywhere in the country'. Since the general atmosphere of social change itself is generative of mobility, moving around in modern conditions in Ashanti 'is a response to the present instability of all social norms which springs in part from the cocoa trade and its resultants, in particular the advent of a money economy'. People move about the more readily if their learning capacity is low, and even cocoa farmers are not tied to one place. (Fortes, 1947, pp. 164–5.) As a more general symptom of restlessness, it is summed up by the Mende proverb that 'one who has not travelled thinks it is only the food cooked by his mother that is sweet' (Little, 1951, p. 259). In the main, however, Western contact having created needs and aspirations impossible to satisfy in the countryside, migration means a flight from the land.

The most primary of these needs is cash, because the acceptability of money as bride-wealth makes it possible for a young man who is enterprising enough to obtain a wife for himself without depending upon father or relatives. More generally, a person requires money in order to live in a 'civilized' way, to buy good clothes, manufactured products, and acquire modern housing. It is also needed for taxes, to pay dues to local associations, to educate oneself or one's children, and so on.

In some areas, the spread of cash crops has increased rural opportunities of earning money. Elsewhere, payment on the farm may still be made partly or wholly in kind, the worker being remunerated by a generous helping of food and drink for his trouble. In the latter case, it is to the towns that men and women migrate not only because wage rates are higher in urban areas and their vicinity, but because there is more chance of regular monetary employment. A steady wage is important partly because of the growing independence of women and their attitude towards marriage. In Sierra Leone, for example, there was a growing preference, even in the 1940's, for some-one who was paid by the month or by the week; farmers whose money came in once or twice during the year were of less interest to them. For this reason, quite a number of the men who would ordinarily remain on the land took a daily job labour-ing in the town during the week and put in what time they could on their farms over the week-end. (Little, 1951, p. 167.)

Opportunities of earning a good income are obviously greater if one has an education; and to be educated improves a person's social standing. This is another reason for young people to move townwards because few secondary schools and facilities for technical training exist outside the larger urban centres. Naturally, the main government offices and business establishments are also located there. Not only does this make urban residence essential for the educated classes in general, but it brings in nearly everyone who is looking for advancement or a 'white-collar' form of employment.

People in the villages send their sons and daughters to urban relatives to be taught a trade or 'minded' while at school, and traders come in to replenish their stock. The fact that there are frequently kinsfolk at hand to receive and house the migrant also adds to the town's attractions. (Balandier, 1955*a*, pp. 40–3.)

Also, closely coupled with these rural practical considerations is the idea of the town being a centre of civilization. Its modern amenities like electric lighting, large stores and shops, cinemas, bars and dance halls have a particularly strong appeal for individuals whose mental horizon has hitherto been bounded by the bush enclosing their village. Even an up-country trading station may be impressive, and his first visit to a small town on the railway line connecting Freetown with the interior prompted a young migrant to say:

I became a sort of idiot as we moved along, for I stood to gaze at whatever English-made articles I have ever seen before, for example, cycles, motor-cycles, and cars. I took a very keen interest in gazing at two-storey buildings, I admired people moving in them, and I often asked my brother whether they would not fall from there. [Little, 1951, p. 260]

For such a person the novel experience of meeting and moving among strangers and the new things he sees have been expressed in the songs of migrants to Ghana. 'Qui n'a pas été à Kumasi, n'ira pas au Paradis', is the refrain. Doubtless it conveys very truly rustic reactions to the relative whirl and bustle of the Ashanti capital.

For these reasons, therefore, many of the younger people move townwards for the sake of adventure. Not only is there apparently much more excitement than in the tribal village, but 'immersion in the town' according to Rouch serves as a modern form of initiation rite. A youth cannot expect to win a girl's favour unless he can show the brand of the town upon him. His return home is a triumph; the *griot* sings his praises and for that day he is the king of his village. (Rouch, pp. 19, 72.)

More prosaically, however, migration is a way of escaping local taxes and court fees and from maltreatment at the hands of an older relative or a husband. Migrants from the Sierra Leone provinces whom Banton interviewed, stressed not only that they could obtain finer things for their money, but that in Freetown they were free from the oppression of the chiefs and elders. In their chiefdoms they were subject to extortion if they showed too much ambition or got into trouble over women; a husband could demand as much as £12 or more for 'woman damage' and would be supported by his chiefs. In Freetown, on the other hand, 'there were plenty of women and everyone looked after himself: many women would take a lover and expect little in the way of presents, while there were others with whom one could have a "short time" for 4s. or 5s.'. (Banton, p. 57.) Similarly, in Stanleyville the village is sometimes thought of nostalgically for the social and economic security of family life and for the abundance of food, but life in the town was said to offer an escape from the 'harsh' authority of tribal chiefs, from sorcery, from drudgery of work in the fields, from obligation to demanding kinsmen and from local hostilities and jealousies of the village.[1] (Douchy and Feldheim, p. 669.)

Cyprian Ekwensi's novels document fairly accurately these attitudes, particularly those of the women. In one of them, *Jagua Nana*, a devotee of the gay life of Lagos is deserted by her lover and falls on evil days. Returning to her own tribe up-country, she is offered security and a good home by an elderly admirer, but the city's hold over her is too strong.

[1] Balandier makes a similar comment, stressing that migration to Brazzaville is partly a method of escaping from tribal culture (1955*b*), p. 42.

Better, from her point of view, the squalor of a Lagos slum
so long as there are sophisticated people around her, the bright
lights of a night-spot, a 'high-life' band, and the chance of
picking up a young and well-to-do patron. (Ekwensi, 1961,
p. 109.) Another of Ekwensi's heroines is so much the 'city' girl
that 'she would be content to walk about a Mayfair-type of
neon-lit shop all day, hang about the city hotels, the ice-cream
bars with not a penny in her handbag, rather than marry a
farmer with a thousand pounds a year for his income, and no
spice of life than the prospect of security and raising children'.
(Ekwensi, 1954, p. 63.)

But other young people abscond and arrive in large cosmopolitan towns like Lagos because their home life is unhappy.
Perhaps a father or a mother has remarried, and the child has
been left to the mercy of an unsympathetic step-parent or
guardian. Motor transport makes escape comparatively easy.
If a runaway finds a relative or friend to provide lodgings so
much the better; if not, he soon learns the trick of living by
his wits and of sleeping at night within a shed at the market or
in some deserted building. (Busia, 1950, p. 96.) So accustomed
do some of these youthful vagrants become to a life of wander-
ing that they eventually lose all sense of home ties and of their
native village. Quite often, the boys become members of
delinquent gangs while the girls generally drift into prostitution.
(*Ibid.*, pp. 84–105.) A youth who is fortunate may manage to
apprentice himself as 'motor boy' to the driver of a lorry.
His job is to service the vehicle, look after passengers, goods,
etc. In return for these services the 'motor boy' is instructed in
driving, provided with lodgings and food, is paid a small daily
wage, and may be able to do profitable trade in vehicle spare
parts as well as earning tips. With the prospects of promotion
to driver it is an attractive opening which draws even literate
youths who have been through school. (Banton, p. 56.)

Since, however, the flight from the land seldom involves whole families it is much easier to speak about the lure of the town than to assess the precise significance of migration as a whole. For one thing, migration is often within the same territory and of a stable reciprocal nature. Also, movements in population are a fairly common phenomenon which has existed between the north and south productive belts of West Africa for centuries. For example, extensive migration exists in Ghana from the adjoining countries of former French West Africa as well as from the northern territories of Ghana itself. According to Rouch's survey there were between 300,000 and 400,000 'French' subjects in Ghana in 1953–4 and at a rough estimate some 600,000 Ghanaians themselves had moved south into Ashanti and the coastal regions. Nowadays, the departure is made without publicity. One of the methods is for four or five migrants to group themselves together, led by an old hand. The only official document necessary is the identity card obtained without any difficulty. The travellers have no luggage, unless it is a plaited straw bag, a cover cloth or a stick. They go to the markets or the town, where they board lorries. (Rouch, pp. 17, 19–20.) In general, migrants are men of twenty to forty-five years, but a large proportion are in the younger age groups. For example, Banton found that 26 per cent of tribesmen registered at the Freetown Employment Exchange were under twenty years and only 15 per cent were over twenty-nine. The ratio of women to men varies with the ethnic group or tribe. Some peoples, such as Hausa, travel with their wives; in other cases, there may be one woman to three or four men. (Rouch, pp. 19, 21, 43; Banton, p. 62.)

Large-scale migration for considerable distances is also seen both in the thousands of Ibo and Yoruba who have moved to Northern Nigeria, and in the movement of Northern Nigerians themselves. Information about some 259,000 of the latter migrants was recorded in a study made in Sokoto Province in 1952–3. It showed that over 60 per cent of them were travelling outside Northern Nigeria, including 17 per cent to Ghana, 18 per cent to Eastern Nigeria, 25 per cent to Western Nigeria, and 2 per cent to French territory. Most of these people are from areas where there is an absence of rain for the greater part of the year. (Prothero.)

Very often, seasonal migration of this kind merely brings about a temporary redistribution of the agricultural population. On the other hand, there is a good deal of evidence that the principal zones of attraction are the large urban centres. In Ghana, for example, the towns of Accra, Takoradi and Kumasi contain only 18 per cent of the total population, but some 40 per cent of the migrants. After them come the mining areas[1] which, in terms of Tarkwa, Prestea, Nsuta and Obuasi, have 10 per cent of the migrants, although containing only 7 per cent of the total population. (Rouch, p. 19.) In the latter towns the tribes principally represented were Moshi, 1,196; Wangara, 604; Kado, 320; and Zabrama out of a total of 19,053 migrants.[2] (Rouch, p. 29.)

The situation is complicated, however, by the fact that many of the migrants do not have any fixed length of stay

[1] It was estimated in 1947 that some 100,000 workers are drawn from foreign territories for employment in the mining districts in Sierra Leone, the Gold Coast, and Nigeria (Firth).

[2] The Moshi are from the Upper Volta in the region of Wagadugu. Under the name of Wangara are known in Ghana all the Mandingo peoples whom one might call the people of Mali; Busanga are from the district of Tenkodogo, Upper Volta; in Ghana the Kado signify the Dogon and the Koromba; the Zabrama designates people speaking the Zerma dialect and includes the people of Songhay. Other important migrant groups are the Hausa comprising all the ethnic groups speaking the Hausa language; the Fulani, otherwise known as the Peulh, who inhabit nowadays Guinea, the Sudan, Northern Nigeria, etc.; the Kotokoli, a group of Moslems of Mandingo origin who are settled in the districts of Sokoto and of Atakpame. (Rouch, pp. 10–12.)

in a particular place. The traders, in particular, spread out round the large centres, to sell the textiles and cheap wares which they have bought, or to buy yams, sheep, etc. According to the Gold Coast Census (1948) in the Colony, Hausas (18,961) constituted the largest group, followed by Moshis (15,156); Kotokoli (14,233); Zabrama (9,808), etc. In Ashanti, Moshis (25,312) constituted the largest group, followed by Wangaras (8,771); Hausa (8,146); Kotokoli (3,172); and Zabrama (1,300).[1]

Furthermore, Rouch's studies suggest that the pattern of migration is not as impermanent in character as has been supposed, but includes settlement. Most of the migrants know where they are going in the first instance. Later on, if they are disappointed in their work they will move on quickly and seek a different place; but the old hands come back each year to the same work, lodging and habits. The migrant stays there until it is time to return home, but if he has not got enough money by March–April, or if his affairs are prospering, he decides to remain for a further year. Enquiry showed that during the period from September to March there were in Accra more than double the number of Zabramas than during the rest of the year. However, length of stay appeared to vary according to ethnic group, and Rouch's figures suggest that relatively few Zabramas stayed as long as two years at a time. The stay of the Gaos and the Kados was similarly short. The Moshis, the Wangaras, and the Fulani tended, on the other hand, to remain for several years, and a relatively large number of Hausas and Yorubas finally settled in Ghana. Also, the better established a person's position, the less likely he was to go. A foreman, a small trader, even a skilled labourer, for

[1] These figures are quoted from the 1948 Census because it has been impossible to obtain a copy of the relevant tables of the 1964 Ghana Census before going to press.

example, dared not leave his place for fear of not recovering it. There were also those who preferred life in Ghana to their own country. However, although the majority of the Hausa were settled, true settlers who never returned home were very rare among the Zabrama, Moshi, or Wangara. Also, whereas formerly a migrant might make a number of journeys to Ghana and then marry and remain there for good, he now probably continued to make a large number of short stays. This was the result of improved transport facilities enabling a person to have two homes, one in Ghana and one in his native country. (Rouch, pp. 19–20.)

Seasonal migration over short distances has also to be included. In Sierra Leone, for example, workers move from the provinces into Freetown after the harvest has been gathered in early January, and again in the rainy season when there is little farm work. These migrants stay only a month or two at a time, their aim being to earn a little money before it is time to return to their village. They usually lodge with relatives, paying for their accommodation with presents bought from the rice harvest. These men travel relatively short distances to reach Freetown; and the evidence in other countries, as well as Sierra Leone, suggests that this is also the case with men and women seeking work of a more permanent kind. (Banton, pp. 60–1.) Thus, about 75 per cent of the population of Lagos are natives of the adjoining Western Region of Nigeria (Census, 1950), and about three-quarters of the inhabitants of Accra were born either there or in southern Ghana (Census, 1948). Quite often, a migrant starts in one of the smaller towns and moves on later to other and larger urban centres.

There is a good deal of variation in the pattern therefore. What is not in doubt is that there has been a rapid increase in the population of areas undergoing industrial development.

Particularly since the 1920's these concentrations of wage-earning urban inhabitants have grown up principally round the ports through which the growing export of primary products pass. For example, since 1921 the population of Dakar has increased from *c.* 32,440 to *c.* 366,000 in 1963,[1] that of Freetown from *c.* 44,000 to *c.* 100,000 in 1960,[2] of Accra from *c.* 38,000 in 1936 to *c.* 338,000 in 1960,[3] that of Lagos from *c.* 99,000 to 450,000 in 1962.[4] A few agglomerations, including some capitals of African chiefdoms, have also developed as interior trading and transport centres in the areas of export crop productions. Thus, Kumasi grew from *c.* 24,000 inhabitants in 1921 to *c.* 190,000 in 1960,[5] and the population of Ibadan which is now given as *c.* 600,000 has more than trebled since 1921.[6] Of smaller towns which have developed for similar reasons, Bo in Sierra Leone increased from *c.* 2,000 inhabitants in 1940 to *c.* 20,000 in 1958,[7] Tamale in the northern region of Ghana from *c.* 4,000 in 1921 to *c.* 40,000 in 1960,[8] while of the new 'mushroom' towns of the Coast, Abidjan in the Ivory Coast increased from *c.* 17,000 in 1937 to *c.* 187,500 in 1960,[9] and Cotonou in Dahomey from *c.* 8,000 in 1931 to

---

[1] Hodgkin, 1956; *Statesman's Yearbook*, 1963. These figures reflect the rate of growth in the former French territories in general. The principal towns of Senegal increased their population by 100 per cent between 1942 and 1952; those of the Ivory Coast by 109 per cent between 1942 and 1952; those in the Cameroons by 250 per cent between 1933 and 1952; those in the Congo by 239 per cent between 1936 and 1952. By comparison the urban population of the Union of South Africa increased by 10·9 per cent between 1936 and 1951. (Balandier, 1955a.)

[2] Buell, *The Native Problem in Africa*, vol. II, 1928, p. 874 and *Sierra Leone Year Book*, 1962.

[3] *Population Atlas of Ghana*, p. 36, and *Handbook of Africa*, 1963.

[4] Buell, *op. cit.* vol. II, p. 646 and *Statesman's Yearbook*, 1963.

[5] *Population Atlas of Ghana*, p. 31 and *Handbook of Africa*, 1963.

[6] Buell, *op. cit.* vol. I and *Statesman's Yearbook*, 1963.

[7] *Sierra Leone Census* 1931 and *Sierra Leone Yearbook*, 1962.

[8] *Population Atlas of Ghana*, p. 27 and *Handbook of Africa*.

[9] Harrison Church, p. 350 and *Statesman's Year Book*, 1963.

c. 54,100 in 1960.[1] In addition, principally as a result of the installation of nearby mines, a number of villages have been converted into towns. Lunsar, in Sierra Leone, for example, a hamlet of 30 people in 1929 grew to some 10,000 inhabitants following the exploitation of iron-ore in its neighbourhood.[2] Enugu, which is now the centre of regional government in eastern Nigeria, originated entirely out of the development of nearby coalfields. Founded in 1914 on an empty site, this town had a population of some 10,000 by 1921[3] which rose to *c.* 82,000 by 1962. Port Harcourt—now Nigeria's second port—was created in turn as a terminus for a railway serving the Enugu coal-fields and it had a population of *c.* 72,000 in 1953.[4]

In part, this rapid growth may be due directly to natural increase because there has been a general rise in the population. For example, in the last twenty years the population of Nigeria has increased at an estimated rate of 1·5 per cent annually and with control of epidemic diseases and improvement in maternity and child welfare, this trend should continue. However, so far as urbanization is concerned, the census figures leave no doubt that migration is the principal factor. Thus, no less than 58 per cent of the population of Lagos consisted in 1950 of people born elsewhere, while from figures provided in the Ghana Census (1960) it may be estimated that only 25 per cent of the population of Takoradi, about 40 per cent of the population of Sekondi, some 37 per cent of the population of Kumasi, and some 47 per cent of the population of Accra are of local origin. In 1948, over one-half the population of Takoradi and 36 per cent in the case of Accra had lived in those towns for less than five years, while in Ghana, as a whole, more than two-thirds of

---

[1] Lombard. [2] Gamble. [3] Hair.
[4] *Nigerian Handbook of Commerce and Industry*, 1962.

the urban inhabitants have been in the towns concerned for less than five years. Modern Freetown, needless to say, has also grown up through migration, but the influx has been spaced over a relatively longer period and it is estimated that one-quarter of all adults of tribal origin and over one-third of their children are of Freetown birth. (Banton, p. 91.)

Sociologically, this rapid urbanization is important for two reasons. Firstly, the fact that so many industrial and other Western ideas and practices are fully assimilated to the African scene makes social change a process of adaptation to new circumstances and conditions. These fresh factors exist because in contrast to the *rus in urbe* characteristic of traditional cities,[1] the 'new' town is mostly a product of forces external not only to itself but to West African society in general. It has grown up mainly in response to the market economy introduced by European colonialism. Though inhabited by Africans, it is largely the creation of Europeans.[2] Its institutions are designed primarily to serve wider, embracing systems of administration and economics, not the indigenous needs of subsistence farmers and craftsmen.

The second point is that migration—the settlement and re-settlement of larger groups of people from the rural areas—creates a far-stretching network of social and other ties between

[1] As typified, for example, by the numerous towns of Yorubaland. In 1931 some 28 per cent of the Yoruba population lived in nine cities of 45,000 inhabitants, while 34 per cent lived in sixteen cities of over 20,000 inhabitants. These towns consist mainly of agriculturists whose farms are made on a belt of land surrounding the city to a depth of fifteen or more miles. Since farming is based largely upon family and kinship, these institutions set the pattern of life in the town which reflects in turn the personal character of relationships in the countryside. There is also a specialized group of weavers, dyers, iron workers, diviners, medicine men who supply all other members with their particular goods and services. Nevertheless, though specialized to an extent which makes each individual economically dependent upon the society as a whole, such a community lacks the degree of specialization of a modern industrial economy. (Bascom, 1955.)

[2] Desch.

the town and the hinterland. It does not necessarily mean a permanent separation between those who have moved and their rural kin. On the contrary, as already described, there is a constant coming and going of traders; and as well as the movement of migrants, townspeople frequently visit or are visited by rural relatives. This happens because migrants frequently return home for ceremonies or to find a wife; others send their daughters to the bush to be educated rather than allow them to grow up in the 'corrupting' influence of the town. Ties are thus maintained with those left at home, and even during their stay in town the migrants send back part of their savings. If married, they contribute to the support of their wives and children: if bachelors, they send remittances to their immediate kin. (Lombard, pp. 364–71; Rouch, p. 136; Balandier, 1955*b*, pp. 203–8.) This means that new ideas and practices acquired by the migrants are transmitted to the countryside. Instead of being confined to the town they are diffused over a much wider area, making the town itself a pace-maker for the larger society.[1]

What, then, distinguishes the new West African town from traditional urbanism is that a large proportion of its population is industrial and depends upon the labour market for a living. The extent of wage-earning varies with the degree of industrialization. In Ghana, which is the most highly industrialized of all four English-speaking countries, it appears to be greatest in Sekondi–Takoradi, where, in 1955, 69 per cent of all families had wage incomes. In Accra (1953), the proportion was 57 per cent, and in Kumasi (1955) 34 per cent. In the last-mentioned town, non-wage incomes, derived mainly from trading and crafts, were the principal source of livelihood, and

[1] A. W. Southall makes a similar comment on the role of the industrialized town in East Africa (cf. Southall, pp. 191–2; and Georges Balandier (1956), p. 506) suggests that the towns, by serving as a field for wider and fuller contacts, acts as a kind of 'laboratory' for the formation of new cultural patterns.

63 per cent of all families were dependent entirely upon these activities. The highest proportion of wage-earning in Sekondi–Takoradi arose from the port and railway activities, while in Accra it was due to employees of the Government and commercial firms and to the port. These findings are based upon surveys of population and household budgets conducted by the Gold Coast Statistical Department which has also investigated wages as a percentage of earnings. During the month of this survey wages constituted 90 per cent of earnings in Sekondi–Takoradi, 67 per cent in Accra, and 22 per cent in Kumasi (1956a, b). What is particularly significant is that migrants made up 40 per cent of the wage earners in Ghana—some 160,000 out of a total of 405,000. They were an important factor in all occupations.

They constituted 98 per cent of the workers employed by the Accra Town Council; 36 per cent of those in the Public Works Department of that city. Seventy-five per cent of the labourers hired by cocoa farmers were from the north, as were also 55 per cent of those working in the mines, 37 per cent of those employed in timber-working and in forestry, 22 per cent of the industrial labour force, 40 per cent of the police, and 20 per cent of the employees of one large commercial concern, the Union Trading Company. They were also independent traders. Thus of 6,096 licensed traders in Accra, 1,649, or 24 per cent were Zabrama. On the ferry at Yedji, an important point on the route of migration, 14,805 out of 35,665 migrants crossing from south to north in March 1954, declared themselves to be traders. [Herskovits, pp. 272–3]

These industrial considerations, including migration, are important for analytical purposes—not because they imply the juxtaposition of different cultures. True, cultural contacts go on—between Westernized Africans and other Africans as well as between Europeans and Africans in general. But the resulting changes are no different from those which occur within a single society. Methodologically, therefore, the problem is not what is 'African', or 'European', or transitional, or in what quantities particular cultural elements exist. The question is what is significant in terms of social groupings and relationships. It is the interaction of the actors—the institutions created by the incoming industrial economy—rather than the cultural components that we have to dissect.

2

TRIBAL ASSOCIATIONS AND SYNCRETIST CULTS

Tribal Associations

A s I shall show later, sociologically, one of the most important of these new institutions inspired and fostered by urbanization is the voluntary association of men and women with economic and other interests in common (Little, 1957, p. 581). Some associational practices and procedures were originally promoted by European missionaries and administrators.[1] The organizations to be described in this chapter are peculiarly the result of migration. Basically, they represent the newly arrived migrants' response to urban conditions. Belonging, in his rural home, to a compact group of kinsmen and neighbours, he has been used to a highly personal set of relationships. He knows of no other way of communal living than this and so to organize similar practices of mutuality is for him a spontaneous adjustment to his environment. Nor in view of the strangeness of his surroundings is it surprising that the migrant often prefers to remain as far as possible in the company of previous associates. The result is that instead of weakening tribal consciousness, life in the new urban environment tends in some respects to make it stronger.

The prototype of this 'super-tribalism' is the Zabrama migrant to Ghana from Niger, who is a single man or, if he is

[1] One of the earliest of these associations was founded in 1787 at Cape Coast by the Rev. Quaque, a leading convert of the Society for the Propagation of the Gospel. This was the Torridzonian Society whose members, Europeans, met weekly for convivial purposes and to open a school to educate twelve Mulatto children (Martin, pp. 294–8).

married, sends his wife back to his home country. He has organized himself in sub-district and village communities which do not allow him to leave his social milieu throughout his whole stay, and has, in his system of chieftainship, transplanted the traditional systems of his native country. Also, not only do the Zabrama migrants remain faithful to their relations with other groups of migrants, to their old enmities and old alliances, but they hold themselves aloof from the native people of Ghana. They take no part in traditional local life except to pay homage to the chief at the Odwira celebration and on other civic occasions.[1] This tendency to isolate themselves exists from the start because Zabrama migrants entering Ghana from the north are, from their departure, members of a single group. If, on their arrival, this group disperses, it is only to form other groups in different places of residence. High rentals and housing shortages force the migrants to share a small room between three, five or ten, and obviously these room mates are always people of the same origin—from the same district if not the same village.[2] The room thus becomes—to use Rouch's graphic expression— 'A little regional cell' where one takes one's meals in common and where in the evenings after work one talks endlessly of one's country. Rouch suggests that this talking at night, *takaneya*, is just as necessary in a sordid shack as in a rural village. (Rouch, pp. 56, 60.)

His apparent rejection of all other groups makes the Zabrama unquestionably the extreme type of migrant. This kind of

[1] Even in public gatherings, such as race meetings, the migrants gather themselves together. One stand at Accra is called the 'Zabrama stand', and one of the cinemas is called the 'Zabrama cinema' (Rouch, p. 59). Fulbe immigrants in Lunsar, Sierra Leone, have held themselves similarly aloof in relations with the other immigrant groups, and they form an entirely separate community on their own (Butcher).

[2] Thus, at the time of Rouch's survey, out of 1500 Zabrama questioned in Accra, 1300 were from a single district—Tillabery, p. 56.

response, however, is a primary reaction and it largely explains why, of all the societies organized by migrants, voluntary associations of fellow tribesmen are often the most common. Ibo migrants who largely originated the movement in Nigeria some thirty years ago are a good example. On moving into the towns of the West and the North they formed associations to protect themselves from the hostile way in which they were received by the local inhabitants when they took jobs as clerks, policemen, traders and labourers (Aloba). Ibos in Lagos at the present day belong to 'meetings' which correspond roughly with the basic social units at home—village, village group, and clan. Those with enough representatives of their own home neighbourhood will hold a 'family' meeting, though members may not be directly related, and the members of this meeting will come from the same cluster of hamlets, which form a 'village'. (Marris.) Marris goes on to report:

One of the Ibo householders interviewed, for instance, belonged to a 'family' meeting which met monthly and raised subscriptions of sixpence a time. Attendance was about thirty, and the funds were used for mutual help in sickness, unemployment, or bereavement. He also belonged to a monthly 'town' meeting—town corresponds with the village group—towns in the Eastern Region are in many cases market and administrative centres rather than concentrations of people, who lived dispersed in their homesteads throughout the area. Any member of the 'family' meeting could also attend the town meeting, where the subscription was 1s. 6d. and attendance over a hundred. [p. 40]

Organizations of this kind are described as ethnic or tribal associations, the French term being *association d'originaire*. They are referred to in this way to distinguish them from associations which also practice mutual aid but where members are united by other factors, such as age, occupation, and education. In fact, although the members of a particular union may speak of themselves as a people from a given region or town, the basis of common origin is often more imaginary than real. As the above example indicates, membership may not be withheld from persons who are not actually affiliated to the particular clan or even the particular tribe concerned. (Caprasse, p. 21.) Tribal associations have not been reported from some of the smaller industrialized towns,[1] but, so far as can be judged, associations are to be found in nearly every urban centre with a large migrant population. There are insufficient figures for wide comparison but the estimation that some 16,900 persons in the municipality of Accra belonged in 1956 to a tribal association suggests the extent of their popularity, particularly as the sex ratio was 1 female to 2·4 males. The largest association had 2,000 members, the smallest 14; thirteen of a sample of thirty-three associations had a membership not exceeding 50, and only seven had a membership over 100. In all, there were ninety-four such tribal associations among twenty-two tribal divisions. Forty-five of these associations were based upon membership of the same tribe, district, or native state, and thirty-five upon the same town. Sixteen unions had their home towns in Nigeria.[2] (Acquah, pp. 105–7.) In samples of householders in central Lagos and on a housing estate, respectively, 30 per cent and 41 per cent belonged to regional associations. (Marris, p. 157.) In Dakar, membership on the basis of occupation ranged between 47 per cent of overseers and 20 per cent of professional men (Mercier, 1956a, p. 522).

The following description of a Fanti union in Takoradi illustrates the general organization:

[1] Such as Lunsar, Sierra Leone. Lunsar has a population of 10,000 of whom nearly 80 per cent belong to the local Temne tribe.

[2] Other tribal groups which have spread internationally are associations of Kru. In Sekondi–Takoradi they have such names as 'Money's Time', 'Excuse me', 'Show your Chemise', and 'High Life'. Nigerian tribal unions have branches in Britain among university students and sea-farers.

All Cape Coast people resident in the town are eligible for membership. There are 300 members on the roll.

The aims of the society are to bring the Cape Coast people in town together, to give members financial assistance when necessary, and to maintain an interest in the welfare of Cape Coast.

The Executive Officers consist of a President, Vice-President, Recording Secretary, Correspondence Secretary, a Financial Secretary, and a Treasurer. There is a separate Finance Board which audits the accounts of the Union.

Members pay a 'Foundation Fee' of 10s. 6d. on admission, and a monthly contribution of 9d.

The Union meets once a fortnight, and all its affairs are conducted in Fanti. A general meeting opens with a hymn and prayer, and closes with a benediction.

When a member dies, the bereaved family receives from the Society a funeral benefit of £7. 4s. When a member's wife, husband, father, or mother dies, the member is given £2. 2s. A sick member receives a sick benefit of 5s.

One of the aims of the Union is to award scholarships to Cape Coast children, but there have not been enough funds to start the scheme.

There are branches of the Union at Takoradi, Tarkwa, Prestea, Bibiani, Bogosu and other places, and the issue of certificates of membership enables a member to transfer his membership to another branch.
[Busia, 1950, pp. 74–5]

It so happens that the majority of the tribal associations in Accra are in practice mere benefit societies. No monetary assistance or other organized help is given to people in the place of origin (Acquah, p. 106). True, mutual aid is the primary function of all such groups (Caprasse, p. 31), but, as the above Fanti union has illustrated, there are also wider interests. In addition to assisting their own members financially, many associations set out to improve their home town, village, or state. Their names—the Calabar Improvement League, The Anlo State Improvement Society, The Igbarra Progressive Union, etc.—reflect this aim. The idea is to provide up-to-date amenities—hospitals, schools, and roads—equal to those of the place into which the migrants have moved. This necessitates a good deal of money-raising.[1] In order, therefore, to encourage members' attachment to their native town or lineage every effort is made to foster and keep alive an interest in the moral beliefs, language, song and history of the tribe. Some associations go so far as to record these things in writing for the benefit of the younger generation who have never known the older customs (Caprasse, p. 34). Social activities include an annual celebration, the organization of dances on festival days and of sports and games for the young people. Some of these unions also produce an annual magazine called an Almanac, in which their members' activities are recorded, and they make a special point of looking after and welcoming persons newly arrived from the country or returned from overseas.

In these ways—through reception committees[2] and by holding 'send-off' parties—they provide a means whereby both the old people and the educated person can maintain contact with their rural relatives and friends (Lombard; Offodile; Achebe).

An important means whereby these improvement unions carry out their objective of bringing 'civilization' to their native towns and villages is through home branches of the associations abroad. These are formed by returning members

[1] However, one of Marris's informants explained that 'We don't send all the money home, we keep the rest in case of any accidents to one of our members—well, you know, either death or trouble. If he comes purposely to borrow money, we give it and tell him not to pay' (p. 41).

[2] Achebe has described fairly accurately, although facetiously, such a reception. 'If Obi had returned by mail boat, the Umuojia Progressive Union (Lagos Branch) would have given him a royal welcome at the harbour. Anyhow, it was decided at their meeting that a big reception should be arranged to which press reporters and photographers should be invited. An invitation was also sent to the Nigerian Broadcasting Service to cover the occasion and to record the Umuojia Ladies' Vocal Orchestra which had been learning a number of new songs' (p. 31).

desiring to continue the comradely spirit they have enjoyed while away. Quite often, local chiefs and other notabilities also help with funds, and the home association embarks on its own regular programme of activities. There are football matches and dances to attract people from the larger towns; and communal work, such as building of bridges, repairing roads, etc., is also undertaken by the union. In Nigeria, the lead in these matters is very often taken by educated persons. The association membership includes all elements on the social, economic and literary scale from peasant to barrister (Coleman, 1958, p. 215). The attitude varies, but among the Ibo affiliation is considered a duty, the shirking of which often results in social ostracism. One of Smythe's informants said: 'You see, we all belong to this [Union] once we come to a city. If you don't, people will say you are not sociable and will not respect you. And, if you didn't join, when you get into trouble, you won't have anyone to help you. So you can see why all of us belong to it.' (p. 30.)

Ethnic unions also include women as members and in some of the Freetown 'family' societies, such as the Kru, women have their own organization.[1] Kru men get a living mainly as sea-farers. In view of the men's absence for long periods, these women's societies play a very important part in the life of this tribal community. The larger of them have 600 to 700 members, and Banton has described the complicated structure which is modelled largely upon the ranks and organization of the ships in which the men serve. The members are divided into three classes: *bor*, *blibli*, and *kafa*.

[1] A few tribal associations are entirely confined to women. In Accra they include the Family Welfare Society, the Ewe women's association and the Kwaku women's association. The first mentioned is run by Akwamu women, and its primary aim is to improve the position of women in family life. It promotes the adoption of destitute children, organizes talks on such problems as drunkenness and gambling, and endeavours to assist the Queen-Mother of the Akwamu State in the discharge of her duties (Acquah, p. 107).

30

The chief officer is the *Wandi* and she has a male counterpart in the *Wambi*. Then, in descending order of importance, come the *Ginah* (derived from 'General' and not 'Engineer' as might have been expected), the *Chape* (Captain), Purser, Judge, Doctor, *Chelenyoh* (the Secretary, Kru word), *Weititunyon* (Treasurer, Kru word), *Massamwi* (Master-at-Arms), *Consabru* (Constable), *Balifru* (Bailiff). Each official has his deputy and the classes have their own representative officers: *bodi*, *bliblidi*, and *kafadi*. A member pays an admission fee of £1. 1s. 0d. and enters as a *kafa*: he or she may subsequently be promoted to a higher class and in this event will be expected to make members of that class a present of several pounds. On the death of a member the representative of his or her maternal kin notifies the society in writing and pays a reporting fee of £1. 2s. 6d. If the deceased was a *kafa* all members contribute 1s.; if he or she was a member of a higher class a *kafa* contributes 3s., a *blibli* 5s. and a *bor* 6s. The relatives of a *bor* are paid £32. 10s. 9d., of a *blibli* £21. 10s. 9d., and of a *kafa* £17. 10s. 8d. For former members of the higher classes this sum is paid out as soon as the report has been authenticated, but the relatives of a *kafa* have to wait until sufficient contributions have come in, and this may take several weeks. [Banton, pp. 188–9]

The men's associations are of a similar type. One men's society instead of grouping its members into classes, divides them according to ships, the members being of equal status. The men's societies tend to favour the paternal kin, and the women's society the maternal, but in the event of the dead member having been a member of more than one society, the two groups of kin may agree to divide their responsibilities.

The above formal arrangements show the way in which clanship has been reorganized. In this modern form a person may be eligible by birth, but active membership requires enrolment. A person can no longer go to a fellow clansman in the expectation of receiving help automatically in the way it was given in the past. The urban version of a clan, therefore, has a new hierarchy of officers and a new set of duties and privileges which are limited to registered members. As the above account makes clear, one of the most important of these benefits is a proper funeral on death.

The following description shows, in addition, how Christian and traditional interests may be merged in the organization of these affairs.[1] The association concerned—a group of Ashanti migrants from Atwima—had its own 'priest' who officiated at the burial of a dead member,[2] taking over after the church service while the mourners were still congregated at the grave-side. Holding one of the emblems of the society, he said:

'Brother we give you good sleep; while on earth, we showed you the way to God with love and unity. Now, we hand you over to the earth, but we humbly ask the Lord that if there is any sin on you, He may forgive you and lead your soul to the place of quietness and peace. Amen.' [Bandoh]

A ceremony for the removal of a dead member's name from the roll of the living followed, spoken in Asante. The members repeated after the priest:

'Almighty God-father, we ask Thee for help, humility and under-standing. We ask Thee to make us know that we are strangers on earth: as strangers, we have no one but Thee, and so make this work of brotherly love which Atwima Brakaum is doing stand firm and last for ever, for the sake of your beloved son, Jesus Christ. Amen.' [*Ibid.*]

There was a further prayer, a hymn, and another prayer was said; this time by the priest alone. Then the head of the association called upon someone who knew the dead man intimately to tell his life history. More speeches followed, and finally the name of the deceased was formally deleted by the head of the association, who said:

[1] Note also Chinua Achebe's description of an Ibo union's meeting (pp. 4–6).
[2] Provided the deceased person was up-to-date with his dues to the society. In the case of a delinquent member, i.e., one who is in arrears, the association pays money to his lineage, but does not perform the usual burial rites for him.

'Brother So-and-So, today is the day we are removing your name from our world in Atwima Society for you to join God's Society. May the Almighty Father help you. Amen.' [*Ibid.*]

The latter examples are all of migrants; but in some cases kin groups have formed associations to protect family interests on the spot. One such Undo (Western Nigeria) group has drawn up a written constitution in booklet form and has an executive committee of which the eldest member is chairman. This association has a full meeting on the first Sunday of every month and there is a monthly subscription; members are entitled to financial benefits from the association when they marry, take a chieftaincy title, die, or send a son to Britain for education. Lands vested in the group can only be alienated by the executive committee. (Lloyd, 1959, p. 60.)

In Accra the members of tribal associations are almost all illiterate and the well educated person, in the main, looks down upon organizations of this kind as parochial and backward looking (Acquah, p. 106). However, it will be clear already that this is not the general attitude. Particularly in the French-speaking countries, educated people have taken the lead in founding and directing ethnic associations. They, and the 'progressive' young men in general, have seen in this resuscitation of the tribal spirit an opportunity of building up much larger structures which may, in turn, be used to bring about social change.

The above-mentioned diffusion of improvement unions to the countryside is one illustration of this developmental process and in Nigeria it underwent three phases of integration. These involved respectively the federation of all branches abroad of the same union; the federation of the federated branches abroad with the home branch; and the formation of an all-tribal federation. The procedure was for members originating from the same region to set up regional bodies to which representatives from the home town and clan associations were elected. These in turn set up the organization covering the whole tribe. Delegates from regional associations sat on the main committee, and once a year at the annual general meeting of this central organization any member could attend. It will thus be seen that the all-tribal federation had a pyramidal structure which began with the primary associations (the extended family among the Ibo and large towns) and passed upwards through the various levels of the social structure (clan), or of the territorial organization (division or province) of the tribe concerned. The first all-tribal federation to be organized was the Ibibio Welfare Union. This occurred in 1928, and since 1947 these larger all-tribal organizations have adopted the name of State Unions. (Coleman, 1952; Acquah, pp. 104–7.)

In view of their comprising every union of members of the same tribe it is not surprising that these Nigerian State Unions have obtained a power and influence far beyond their original objectives. They have played a particularly important part, for example, in the expansion of education. They ran their own schools and offered scholarships for deserving boys and girls. In some places, the monthly contribution of members for education was invested in some form of commercial enterprise, and appeals for money to build schools seemed to meet with an extremely ready response. One observer claimed that he saw an up-country union raise in six hours and in a single meeting over £16,000 for such purposes. Higher education has also been provided. In 1938, for example, the Ibibio State sent eight students, all in one day, to England and America, and several leading members of the Nigerian Eastern House of Assembly owe their training in British universities to State Union money. (Aloba.) Even more ambitious plans have included the building of a national bank where people can

34

obtain loans for industrial and commercial purposes; and, in this connection, some unions have economic advisers who survey trade reports for the benefit of members (Offodile).

Syncretist Cults

Tribal associations, comprising individuals with a common interest in their place of origin, keep the migrant in touch with his own people, and help him with mutual benefit schemes. These, however, are not his only needs. He may indeed eschew the companionship of people outside his own tribe, but in a multi-tribal community some adjustment to strangers is unavoidable, if only at work. Especially if the migrant is a trader, success in business will depend upon an amicable relationship not only with his customers but with fellow traders. Moreover, life in the town—the experience of meeting fellow tribesmen who have prospered, of participation in new activities, of witnessing fresh sights—creates further interests and needs which are the more readily generated because of the original impulse to migration itself. In West Africa today, a young man or woman does not require the stimulus of school education to arouse ambition. Social change is multifarious enough to suggest ways in which even an illiterate person can better him or herself.

In addition, therefore, to tribal companionship and protection, newcomers to the town have needs which are more specifically related to their business or occupation, to their personal ambitions, to recreation, and also to religion. They form further associations to cater for these interests—associations which are designed to serve the freshly awakened aspirations of their members but are basically traditional in spirit and practice.

The latter is the case because, excepting the as yet small school-educated section of the population, town dwellers in general retain much of their previous outlook. They continue to dress, speak, prepare their food, and to interact socially largely as they did in their rural villages or before their town was industrialized. Quite often the modern growth of houses, offices, churches and shops has displaced very little of the original scene. Either such buildings cluster conspicuously apart, as bright new residential zones for wealthier Africans and Lebanese as well as Europeans, or else they line the frontages of the old streets like concrete dams blocking the indigenous tide of life welling behind them.

And, there are some striking contrasts. That large, solidly-built house opposite the bank is the home of a prosperous African barrister. He and his wife and their grown-up daughter have all had professional training in England. Excepting the fact that they speak a native language as well as English, their general habits and outlook are Western rather than African—down to minor details of etiquette. The house itself is spacious, furnished and decorated in a way which would find favour with the most well-to-do inhabitants of a London suburb. There is electric light, a refrigerator, modern plumbing in the bathroom, and the water closet has a flush system. Behind this house, however, in a side street, are other houses—very often mere shacks. These have been constructed mainly out of sheets of tin, wooden boarding, and strips of sacking and cloth. They provide shelter for a number of individual households using the common yard, or compound, which these cabin-like structures enclose. In the latter open, mud-surfaced space, domestic utensils are littered. In addition to mortars and pestles, there is a shrine to the ancestral spirits in front of which the remains of a recent sacrifice—the feathers of a cock and some rice—are scattered.

In other words, although the working lives of the town's inhabitants are mechanized—they drive and use lorries as a matter of daily routine—the ancient ceremonies are not neglected. Even among Christians and educated people there is still a good deal of faith in the ancient religions and in the use of magical media, charms and talismans. Fiawoo, for example, examined by questionnaire 164 pupils at secondary schools in eastern Ghana, of whom all but one were Christian and had Christian parents (1956*b*).[1] Only 37 per cent of his sample thought it superstitious to believe in ghosts; only about 16 per cent disbelieved in the reality of witches and about 43 per cent of the believers claimed personal experience; 15 per cent felt that native medicine is more efficacious than modern medicine and 34 per cent had at one time or another consulted ritual specialists on personal matters such as sickness, reclaiming lost property, and acquiring 'intelligence' at school (*ibid.*).

Certain cults, however, like those of the Komo of the Bambara, the masked dances of the Dogon, and the Poro of the Mende are difficult to transport. Since their prohibitions cannot be enforced among a multi-tribal population, the sacred spirits no longer make a public appearance in the larger towns. The result is that the various cults brought in by the migrants have been adapted to local conditions. For example, both the Atike movement and Tigari introduced respectively into eastern and southern Ghana have incorporated Christian and Islamic elements. The word *Atike*[2] implies therapeutic medicine and so the function of these cults is to cure by means of supernatural power, or *vodu*. One of them—Blekete or Nana

[1] It was not possible to ascertain the 'reality' of the Christian status of students. The only criteria here were Baptism and Confirmation. Whether the students professed Christianity and also belonged to indigenous cults was not known. Messenger, too, reports of the Anang that no matter how Europeanized a person may be, he usually is able to recount his numerous experiences with *ifot* and ghosts, and can recite the Anang rationale for their existence (p. 299).

[2] The word is synonymous with *ama*, or processed herb, generally regarded as indispensable in the therapeutic, and non-therapeutic prophylactic charms and amulets (Fiawoo, 1959*b*).

Kunde—has been known in Anlo, eastern Ghana, for over a quarter-century. In Blekete the character of this *vodu* is determined by two major 'god' forms, male and female respectively, and a minor female 'goddess'. These are symbolized by various ritual objects, the most representative being kola-nuts and herbs, wooden stools, spears, and the skulls of a dog, cow, or cat. There are several officials, including a priest, who is training in the slaughter of sacrificial animals, in special types of dancing, and in the use of herbs. (Fiawoo, 1959*b*.)

These syncretist cults attract many devotees, largely because they claim to cure and protect against sickness of both natural and supernatural causation. Illness may sometimes be traced to the displeasure of the lineal ancestors, and in this case the appropriate propitiatory rites pacify the spiritual agents and restore the patient to health. But recovery or normality is not so rapidly assured when evil spirits, including witchcraft, are believed to be the cause of illness. Such evil influences are supposedly at the back of family disasters, such as the successive death of one's children and sterility, as well as making it impossible for modern medicine to work effectively. The cult is believed capable of reaching the heart of the disease, i.e., by the apprehension of the evil spirits at the back of it. It also claims to offer complete protection against jealous rivals and the machination of bad spirits. The only prerequisite for members enjoying the full benefit of this insurance is that they make a clean breast of their past life. (Fiawoo, 1959*b*.)

Generally, the shrine is located outside the town and there are regular celebrations on Sunday afternoons. Members, including clerks, semi-literate mechanics, and artisans, assemble there for four or five hours of continuous drumming, singing and dancing. Membership is open to children accompanied by their parents as well as to men and women. There is no period of preparation or prolonged initiation. One simply signifies one's interest and preparedness to abide by the rules, and conform to the decorum of membership. Then follows the brief ritual of *atikedudu* or 'eating the medicine'. Kneeling before the priest and the Blekete altar, the would-be neophyte makes the following declaration: 'I dedicate myself to you, Nana, and your services. Help my children to live; save my family from evil influences.' The priest shares with the initiate a kola-nut which has been sanctified at the altar. The chewing of the nut and the shake of hands receives the initiate into full membership, and he is then given preliminary instruction in the taboos or rules he must observe as a member.[1] Most of these rules are in the nature of moral precepts, not unlike the Ten Commandments of the Old Testament. The following is an English rendering, a free translation of the vernacular version:

1. Honour your father and mother.
2. Do not impulsively decline the meals of your parents or wife (or wives).
3. You must not commit murder.
4. You must not bear false witness against anyone. To profess to see what has not been seen is gross dishonesty.
5. You must not steal.
6. You must not covet your neighbour's property or his wife.
7. Each member—male or female—is expected to marry according to the rules of the cult.
8. If sickness brings you to Blekete, make a clean breast of all your sins, and your health is assured.
9. Abortion is a criminal act, tantamount to murder. An abortionist shall be subject to the following penal restitution: a ram, a dog, a guinea-fowl, two fowls, two pigeons, a sum of five pounds, three

---

[1] Children under ten years of age received into membership may also 'eat the medicine', but without the vows to Blekete. Later, when they have attained maturity and are able to discern right from wrong, they are invited by the priest for re-initiation, when the whole ritual is gone over and the taboos enjoined as for adults.

pans of kola-nuts, three bottles of liquor. Failure to make full restitution means death at the hands of Blekete, for the wages of sin is death.

10. Do not indulge in falsehood for it is vicious. An impostor shall make atonement with three pans of kola-nuts (each pan of twenty-four nuts) and three bottles of liquor.

11. No devotee shall practise witchcraft, nor malign another as a witch.

12. It is the duty of members to help others, alert those in imminent danger and extricate those in difficulties.

13. Members of Blekete are enjoined to pray for the well-being of mankind, including their enemies.

14. Women in attendance at prayer must remove their shoes and head-dress.

15. Men in attendance at prayer must remove their hats and shoes and pipes. Failure to comply is gross irreverence for Blekete. One bottle of liquor, a pan of kola-nuts and a sum of six shillings shall be exacted from offenders.

16. Members must remember Sunday and make it a day of prayer.

17. No female devotee shall entertain indecent sex-play, as for example, cohabitation out of doors.

18. Similarly, it is reprehensible for a male member to make sexual advances to a woman out of doors.

19. Divorce, unless sanctioned by the cult, is prohibited. Each approved divorce shall have been most fully examined by the entire cult membership. In the event of divorce, the bride-wealth—as fixed by the cult—shall be restored. Bride-wealth according to cult specification, includes a dog, a ram, two yards calico, a mat, a sum of £2. 10s. 0d., three bottles of liquor, three pans of kola-nuts.

20. No member shall seek the help of a diviner (boko) to be rid of witches, let alone be prevailed upon to make offerings (vosasa).

21. To be haunted by witches is a sign of supernatural disfavour. In such predicament, it is expedient to make full confession to Blekete, who has absolute power over such influences.

22. You must not be stingy.

23. Do not feed on the carcass of any animal.

24. Do not feed on pork.

25. You must not kill the viper (fli) because it is an Awusa (Hausa) deity.

26. Dissatisfied members may withdraw from active membership when they please.

27. Do not forswear or mention *Kunde* in vain. Perjurors shall be subject to the following restitution: a dog, a ram, a cat, two fowls, two pigeons, three pans of kola-nuts, three bottles of liquor, a sum of five pounds. The criminal must pay for his crime.

28. No member shall be gainfully employed on Sunday.

29. It is malicious for a member to malign or entertain base suspicions of another.

30. Devotees in need should feel free to speak their minds to Blekete in prayer and also make commensurate pledges. Such pledges must be redeemed as soon as goals are attained.

31. Votaries are expected to pay annual dues towards an annual feast at the close of the calendar year. Delinquent members shall stand trial before a court of fellow members, and if their conduct warrants it, shall be expelled from cult membership. [Fiawoo, 1959*b*]

The content of membership rules at once suggests a heterogeneous cultural background with corresponding religious accretions. On the one hand we see northern Ghana, Fanti, Anlo and possible Western European cultural elements; on the other we see indigenous African religious beliefs and practices to which Christian and Moslem elements have been grafted. Rules 14 and 15 which prohibit shoes and headdresses in the Blekete 'temple' are reminiscent of Islamic practices. So is the avoidance of pork as an item of diet (rule 24). The rule against stinginess (rule 22) may reflect Moslem almsgiving enjoined on all the 'faithful'. Nor are the Christian components hard to delineate. The first few injunctions are not unlike the Ten Commandments of the Old Testament: 'Thou shalt not kill, thou shalt not steal, honour thy father and thy mother, remember the Sabbath day', etc. The emphasis on the observance of Sunday as a day of prayer and freedom from gainful employment is strikingly similar to Christian tenets. The Christian ethical doctrine of 'my brother's keeper' is most adequately exemplified in the injunctions to pray for mankind, including one's enemies, to alert those in danger and not to cherish evil thoughts of others. However, the fame of Blekete as pre-eminently qualified to cure cases of witchcraft and dispel witches, as well as the general set-up, will readily suggest features of an indigenous African religious cult, which, in fact, it is. (Fiawoo, 1959b.)

On the purely cultural level, the kola-nuts, the injunction against the killing of the viper, as well as the 'toga' worn by the priest, the drums and some of the percussion instruments are definitely of northern Ghana extraction. The terms 'Nana' and 'Mena' are of Fanti lineage; they are honorific terms, the equivalents of grandfather or chief and old lady respectively. On the Anlo cultural side of the ledger, filial respect (amebubu), the kernel of education in every home is amply reflected; the taboos on murder, false witness, theft, dishonesty, adultery are not unlike the Nyiko taboos discussed in the traditional background. Similarly, the injunction against indiscreet sex relations, the return of the bride-wealth where the woman seeks divorce are the direct expressions of local observances. In the absence of a national festival comparable to the Akan 'Akwasidae' and 'Wukudae' or 'Anwonada',[1] Easter and New Year (particularly the latter) are lustily celebrated. In the field of ritual specialization, the form and structure of Blekete priesthood is substantially identical to indigenous Anlo practice. (Fiawoo, 1959b.)

Ward has described a slightly different form of cult which had its shrine not far from Kumasi. The 'medicine', or 'fetish' (as Ward terms it) to which the shrine[2] belonged was called

[1] These are traditional Akan forty-day festivals which have been adopted by related medicine cults in Akan areas.

[2] Most shrines are privately owned but some are purchased by a community and set up by permission of the chief as a new power to protect the town against the growing incidence of witchcraft, stealing, marital infidelity, and the unrest brought about by the changing times (Field, p. 183).

Kune. *Kune* came from the Northern Territories and was served by a priest dressed in northern costume and following a northern ritual of slaughtering small fowls. The priest was attended by four priestesses, the chief of whom was his classificatory sister. All these people could suffer possession when, as the people said, 'the powers came upon them'. Any one could become a cult member, or a member of the 'fetish', by paying a small sum, taking a ritual bite or two of kola, and undertaking to obey the fetish rules. The rules appear to be very similar to those of Atike—'Do not commit adultery'; 'Do not swear against thy neighbour'; 'Do not steal'; 'Do not harbour evil thoughts against anyone', and so forth. Similarly, membership of the fetish was sought for protection against witchcraft and sorcery, particularly by barren women or those whose children were continually sick or dying, by impotent men, by anyone sick of an apparently incurable disease, by those who had any reason to fear economic failure or failure in examinations, all of which misfortunes are ascribed to the evil intentions of others. (Ward, pp. 52–3.)

These new 'witch-finding cults' as they have been called in the context of Ashanti have been likened to Tigari, but according to Christensen there are some differences. Unlike the Tigari priests, the individuals who establish their own cults rarely served an apprenticeship. Also, Tigari and similar movements have a wider function. In addition to 'catching witches' they deal with securing jobs, economic gain, or protection while travelling. Not only those who fear 'witches' join the cult, for many members regard it as an insurance against any danger, including not only the so-called pagan, but also the literates, Christians and Moslems. (Christensen, p. 277.)

Various neo-Christian prophetic or messianic movements attract adherents for similar reasons. One of the most notable was named after William Wade Harris, a Grebo by origin, who was born in Liberia. He travelled through what was then French West Africa and the Gold Coast preaching against fetish, lying, strong drink and adultery. After Harris's death the cult dwindled but it later revived and became widespread in the Ivory Coast, particularly Abidjan. Baptism and funeral rites were its most important rituals. Numerous other prophetic cults included that of Deima, founded by a Godi woman. The prophetess, who had been baptized a Protestant, had an encounter with a serpent through whom she acquired ashes and water endowed with miraculous power of protecting believers from all disease. Devotees could obtain a supply of this medicine for a few francs, but if they harboured any bitterness in their hearts while drinking it they might fall ill or even die. Membership of the cult itself was open to any one prepared to renounce his present religion and to swear not to injure his neighbours by poison or sorcery. (Holas, 1954.)

A more militant form of messianic movement was founded in the Lower Congo by Simon Kimbangou, a Christian catechist. He claimed to have been sent by God with a special revelation for the African race. He was arrested in 1921 and deported by the Belgian authorities, but the idea that he would return as the 'saviour and king of black people' and liberate them from the Colonial yoke was kept alive and gave rise to quite an elaborate organization of syncretistic churches. The claim specially made for Kimbanguism and the other dogmas deriving from it was that they represented a spiritual achievement on the part of the Africans comparable to the major religions of other races. The picture held out was of a new order, coinciding with the African church, which would be a political as well as a religious system. Kimbanguism represents a fairly typical reaction to the colonial situation in the Congo. What, however, is significant is that the Christian ideal of

44

brotherly love was part of its system and was advocated as a means of overcoming ancient tribal enmities and barriers of clanship. Traditional magico-religious practices, with the exception of the ancestral cult, were condemned. An attempt was also made to meet the new conditions by limiting polygyny to two or three wives; and adultery and the taking of alcohol, as well as thieving, were proscribed. Sunday, and a number of other special days were to be observed; converts had to make confession in public; the sexes were segregated during services; and above all, marriage with a non-member of the church was forbidden. (Balandier, 1953; Comhaire, 1955.)

Finally, mention should also be made of the numerous heterogeneous 'church' groups which have developed a type of worship and an ethos compounded on Christian and indigenous elements. These are sects which have split away from, or sprung up in relative independence of, the older mission churches. Some of these 'churches' model their organization on the pattern of the Protestant or Roman Catholic missions from which they have seceded, but permit polygamy. In others, emphasis is placed upon the 'prophet' or 'leader' of the sect who was called to found the church. Also prominent is the revivalistic character of their worship which includes speaking with tongues, spirit possession and the interpretation of dreams and visions. In the services there is complete congregational participation in the form of hand-clapping, dancing, and sometimes drumming, spontaneous singing and pious ejaculation. Other common elements include a special interest in faith-healing, in the exorcism of malevolent spirits by prayers, fastings, sprinkling with 'holy' water, and anointing with oil. In one of these sects in Ghana, every new member is baptized by sprinkling and the laying-on of hands following his public confession of sins; he or she is then given a new 'heavenly' name by the prophet. All members wear a small wooden crucifix around the neck and are obliged to fast every Friday, taking only water and chewing kola from dawn until dusk; longer fasts up to seven days are prescribed for the clergy. There is a taboo on sexual intercourse and on indecent conversation during fast-periods. Alcohol, tobacco, pork and 'blood' are forbidden, and menstruous women do not join in services of worship, although their participation is not forbidden. Members are not allowed to consult either Western-trained doctors or African herbalists, and resort to a medicine man or to magical healing of any kind is punishable by prompt exclusion from the church. (Parrinder, pp. 107–32; J. Noel Smith; Baeta.)

3

MUTUAL AID AND RECREATION

Mutual Aid

MIGRANTS who have left behind their rural villages and families are confronted by a more impersonal system of relationships than exists at home. It operates through the economic laws of supply and demand but offers as yet few of the safeguards of a modern welfare state. There is no scheme of social insurance to cover sickness or disability and no pension scheme for widows, orphans and old people, nor is there any national assistance to provide for the destitute or the unemployed. Ethnic associations alleviate these drawbacks to some extent, but their provision of mutual aid only covers a limited number of contingencies. Nor does a tribally based system meet the needs of people earning their living under industrial conditions. True, there is a tendency, for historical reasons, for certain occupations to be mainly the province of particular tribes, and a few tribes have a virtual monopoly of some minor types of trade.[1] But the general situation is that

[1] Accra may be cited as an example. The latest figures are not available at the time of writing, but the 1948 census showed that the majority of farmers and fishermen were Gas and Adangmes. The manufacturing industries comprised, for the most part, workers recruited from the tribes of southern Ghana and Ashanti. In the building trades tribes from southern Ghana predominated, followed by tribes from Ashanti. In transport, although these two broad divisions provided the bulk of the workers, tribes from northern Ghana and from outside Ghana provided a higher proportion than they did in the other industrial groups mentioned above. These northern tribes figure, however, much more prominently in commerce, public service, and in occupations not specifically defined. In personal service, largely domestic work, tribes from outside Ghana provided the greatest proportion (Acquah, pp. 65–6). In Kumasi, the yam trade was for many years almost entirely in the hands of the Gas, and in most of the towns of Ghana the great majority of itinerant petty traders are Zabramas (Rouch, pp. 37–8).

the principal activities of the town—commerce, administration, transport, mining—are organized irrespective of tribe. In the main, economic considerations alone—the demand for special skills and forms of training—determine who the workers are.

These facts account for the wide incidence of associations concerned with mutual benefit or with the furtherance of occupational aims. They also explain why in these organizations the economic interest of their members is the primary purpose of association. In Accra, for example, benevolent thrift societies claim to be open to all without regard to tribe or religion. Some of these organizations had been in existence for more than 30 years when they were studied in 1954, and they had a total membership between them of 26,193. All of them gave assistance to members in sickness and bereavement and donated sums of money to the kinsfolk of a deceased member. In addition, some gave assistance to members when they were robbed, involved in a court case, and at the birth of a child. These societies were also in the habit of providing a lump sum to each member in rotation. This form of capital raising provides a ready sum of money which can be used to acquire goods for trading, to build a house, or to obtain some other desired object. (Acquah.) One of the best known is Nanemei Akpee (Society of Friends) which has branches in several Ghana towns and is supported by influential patrons. Its motto is 'Love is the Key', i.e. the key which opens the door to brotherhood. (Acquah, p. 87.)

This society has a more comprehensive and generous scheme of benefits than most similar associations. For example, it donates a guinea on the birth of a member's child, provided the father or mother concerned has proved a satisfactory member and has been on the books for at least six months. This donation is repeated on the arrival of each fresh child, the children being looked upon as prospective members of the society. Individual members also give quite substantial gifts of money or toys at the 'outdooring' ceremony which takes place eight days after birth. There are the usual sick benefits, and on the death of a member about £10 is given to his or her family, this sum being raised by a compulsory levy of 1s. on every member. The society also lends furniture and other equipment for the wake, contributes a guinea to the expenses of a memorial service, and delegates twelve members to attend it in order to console the deceased's relative and serve him with bread and tea. The society does not pay for a memorial service, however, in the case of a pagan's burial. Nanemei Akpee also comes to the aid of a member whose property has been stolen and may even find ways of helping members in grave financial difficulty. On one occasion, for example, the society arranged for two of its well-to-do members to make an interest-free loan of £500 to another member in danger of being imprisoned for having embezzled this sum from a trading firm. The society's own funds depend upon an entrance fee of 5s. and weekly dues of 3d. per member, but it may appeal to its members for a special contribution in the event of financial difficulties of its own. The amount levied per head is fixed by the committee after discussion at a general meeting. Dances, jumble sales and bazaars are also organized as further methods of raising money. (Bandoh.)

Since, however, the great majority of Nanemei Akpee's members are market women keen to obtain working capital, its most important function is to help its members obtain loans and to save. This is done by holding meetings once every week at which a collection is taken. All the women present give as much money as they feel they can afford and their contributions are written in the book supplied to each member for this purpose and containing her number and name. The officials receiving this money also have a list of the society's members in order of seniority, depending upon the date on which they have joined. When the collection is finished, all the money is given to the member whose name has the first place on the list; the following week it is given to the second, then to the third, and so on. Eventually, all members will in this way receive a contribution, though the process as a whole naturally takes a very long time. The man or woman who receives a collection of money is also given a list showing the amount of money contributed by other members. This determines during later months the amounts of money he must contribute himself. For example, if A has given B two shillings, then B must raise at least the same amount when eventually A's turn arrives to receive a weekly collection. The person whose turn it is to receive also knows how much is due to him from individual members because the amounts that he has contributed have all been recorded in his book. (Carey.)

At meetings, the women wear a smart white uniform and there is community singing, usually of Christian hymns. The members sit in two main groups: those who have already received collections, on one side, and those whose turn is still to come, on the other. Between them sits the member whose turn it is at that particular meeting. Before taking her place in the meeting, however, each member first reports to the officials receiving and recording the contributions. The latter sit in couples facing the meeting and by each table there is a bucket into which the money is dropped. As explained above, if the member concerned has already been 'aided' she hands over the amount that the person receiving the collection that day donated to her. If not, she contributes as much as she likes or feels she can afford. In effect, this arrangement means that senior members, i.e., those who have joined early, receive an interest-free loan, which they repay weekly by small instalments; those at the bottom of the list, on the other hand, are saving in a small way, for their own ultimate benefit. In a period of rising prices, those on the top of the list naturally have the advantage, but on the other hand those who wait longer may receive more because the society's membership will in the meantime have increased. The system is also fairly elastic, and if a member urgently needs cash, perhaps because of some business or domestic crises, she may be allowed to jump the queue of weekly subscriptions, and so receive her collection before she is entitled to do so. This provides a very useful alternative to negotiating a private loan. The average yield of the collection in a Kumasi branch is said to be within the neighbourhood of £70, representing contributions from about 300 members out of a total membership of some 600. (Carey.)

The above method of raising capital has been described in detail because it apparently originated in a traditional practice. The institutions concerned have been termed 'rotating credit associations' (Geertz), and as a means of assisting small-scale capital formation they exist widely throughout the world.[1] Known as *esusu* among the Yoruba, they are found in various parts of West Africa with slightly different names, e.g. *asusu* in Freetown; *susu* in Kumasi; *osusu* among the Ibibio of south-eastern Nigeria;[2] *adaski* among the Hausa of Northern Nigeria;[3] *djana* among the Fang of the southern Cameroon;[4] *ndjonu* in Dahomey;[5] *bandoi* in Leopoldville;[6]

[1] In addition to England, where they are known as 'Christmas' clubs or 'slate' clubs, their geographical range includes China, Malaya, Java, Sarawak, Vietnam, India, South Africa, etc. (Ardener, Shirley, *The Comparative Study of Rotating Credit Association*, unpublished MS).

[2] Jeffreys, M. D. W., 'Le associazoni "Osusu" nel' Africa occidentale', *Revista di Etnografia* (1951).

[3] Smith, M. G., pp. 1–20.

[4] Pauvert, p. 89.

[5] Guilbot.

[6] Comhaire-Sylvain, 1950a, p. 101.

and *tontines* in Porto Novo.[1] Traditionally, Yoruba *esusu* groups seem to have been restricted very largely to men and women as members of the same compound.[2] In more general terms, however, membership of these associations may be based on one or more criteria, including sex and age as well as kinship. Nowadays, not only do many of the benevolent societies have the system in addition to their mutual benefit schemes, but *esusu* groups are frequently organized among people working in the same office, workshop or school, and among market women. When the group concerned is a simple association of friends or acquaintances with a common interest in raising funds for business it can be argued that *esusu* is a club, but many *esusu* groups hold no meetings and the members frequently are not known to one another.

Contribution clubs among the Mba-Ise Ibo of south-eastern Nigeria apparently represent a quite sophisticated development

---

[1] Tardits, p. 36.

[2] Basically, 'the *esusu* is a fund to which a group of individuals make fixed contributions of money at stated intervals; the total amount contributed by the entire group is assigned to each of the members in rotation'. The number of contributors, the size of the contribution and the length of the intervals at which they are made vary from one group to another. For example, suppose twenty members were to contribute 1s. each, monthly. At the end of twenty months, which completes the cycle in this case, each member will have contributed 20s. and will on one occasion have received this amount in return. There is neither gain nor loss, but the advantage to the members is that they have available a large sum of money with which to make expensive purchases or to meet debts of considerable size. Furthermore, an attempt is made to pay the fund to members at times when they have special need of it. Anyone who wishes to do so may found an *esusu* group, provided that the others are willing to entrust their money to him. He simply announces his proposal to his friends, and those who wish to join indicate their intention. They, in turn, inform their acquaintances of the proposed *esusu*, thus drawing additional members into the circle. The larger groups are divided into four or more sub-groups or 'roads' (first, second, third, fourth) according to the order in which they receive the fund, which is rotated among the sub-groups in turn. Friends of the founder who have applied directly to him for admission become heads of the 'roads' and may be made responsible for collecting the contributions and making the disbursement within their sub-groups (Bascom, 1952, pp. 63–4).

52

of the basic system. According to Shirley Ardener, such a club meets every eight days, i.e., once every Ibo week. Membership is open to men or women, and the body of members is divided into seven sections, each under a headman. Each member pays one or more weekly subscriptions. The money collected from members goes straight from their pockets to the pocket of the recipient member for that week. This is an important factor in the stability of these clubs, for there is no possibility of it being lost, stolen or embezzled before it reaches its proper destination. The recipient takes the amount collected and signs or thumb-prints a receipt, promising to continue to pay his share until every other member has, in turn, received his take-out. A senior man from the recipient's compound must sign a guarantee that he will continue to pay the members' shares in the club should the recipient fail to do so himself. These statements are witnessed and kept by the club secretary, and in court proceedings they are upheld by the native bench. The recipient is also required to supply six calabashes of palm wine for the refreshment of the club members at the meeting and to put 4s. of his take-out into a club box. This box fund is used partly for letting small amounts out on loan to members.[1] (Ardener, 1953, pp. 128–42.)

These Ibo contribution clubs fall roughly into four groups. The first group comprises those in which the headmen belong to the same local unit. Another type is that in which the organizers belong to a professional or trade group; and a third type of club is that which is organized within an existing association. An association such as the Yam Title-Society or an

---

[1] A further method of obtaining money is for a member to borrow from a private individual and sign an agreement handing over his rights to his take-out when it falls due. He must continue, of course, to pay his shares in the club. As well as signing over rights to his take-out for a cash loan, a member must also do so in order to acquire certain consumer goods, such as a bicycle. Both such transactions must be witnessed by the headman (Ardener, 1953).

age-grade may often be in a position to provide this, and membership may or may not be confined to members of the association. Lastly, there are those contribution clubs which are organized by women. (Ardener, 1953.) Quite often there is a series of officials such as Council members for judging real or fictitious disputes during meetings; Council Messengers to call witnesses; Checkers to count the money; Dividers to share the wine and food between members; Food Tasters and Sanitary Officers to adjudge the quality of the food, and so forth (*ibid.* pp. 132–3).

In addition to their economic interests, mutual benefit societies generally have social activities, and those of the Ghanaian associations mentioned above are fairly typical. They include excursions and picnics; concerts, singing, dancing and drumming; religious talks and discussions, literacy classes, debates, and cinema shows; first-aid services; initiation ceremonies for new members; and the laying of wreaths on graves of former members. The expense is met out of regular dues which pay for such things as rent, lighting, books, stamps, cups, forms, flags, banners, drums, messengers, tables, and in some cases, honoraria to secretaries. In addition, collections are made for money required for the various forms of assistance rendered to members, and for the help which more than half the societies studied extend to the wider public, especially the socially handicapped. Members take presents of money and in kind to hospitals and prisons and to other institutions where the inmates may be in need of advice or encouragement. (Acquah, pp. 87–91.)

The constitution and by-laws of one of these societies provides an indication of their organization in general. This society—Yehowa Kpee (Society of God)—has a president and seven or eight other officials each of whom has his own duties in the administration. Yehowa Kpee's primary aim is 'to foster the spirit of friendship amongst its members'. It also undertakes to help its members with their financial and other problems and to arrange for them to receive medical treatment from a particular doctor in Accra. Members are expected not only to pay their dues and attend meetings of the society punctually and regularly, but to refrain from disorderly behaviour both in the society and outside it in the town. All these matters are the subject of disciplinary rules which include the society's right to expel a member if he refuses to mend his conduct after being warned a number of times. A member absenting himself from meetings for three consecutive months without permission is suspended and is not readmitted to the benefits of membership until he has made up all his arrears of dues. (Acquah, pp. 90–91.)

In Freetown, friendly societies of a somewhat similar kind are very popular among the Creole people, and some of these slightly resemble tribal unions in being groups of common ancestry. For example, there are the Nova Scotia and Maroons Descendants Associations, the Popo Maintenance Society, and another is called the Hand to Mott Society, transcribing the Creole pronunciation of 'mouth'. In addition to the tribal associations themselves, the Moslem section of the tribal population also run societies of a benefit nature and the congregations of the mosques usually have what is loosely called a *Jama compin* (*compin* being the Creole word for 'company'). The secretary of the *Jama* keeps a list of contributors, who pay 6*d.* per head on the death of any member's relative. (Banton, pp. 187–8.) In the *bandoi* (see p. 51) membership is open to all adults and children of the same Christian name. This type of association was introduced to Leopoldville by Up-River people. Subscriptions vary between two and five francs, depending on the commonness of the name; and therefore on the number of members. Assistance is given by the association at weddings, or, at the death of members, to their families. (Comhaire-Sylvain, 1950*a*.)

As will be gathered from the figures quoted above groups concerned with mutual benefit and helping their members to save have a very large female membership. A number of them, of course, consist entirely of women. An example, reported in 1955, was the Bo United Moslem Women's Society in Sierra Leone. This collected a small weekly subscription, and persons joining as new members had to provide the equivalent of what a foundation member had already paid in subscriptions. This money was used to help members who were ill or who had expenses in connection with the burial of a relative: some of it was also disbursed as alms. The leader of the society was the Mammy Queen, the holder of this office being an elderly woman who spoke the languages of at least six of the tribes locally resident in the town. There were a number of additional officials, part of whose duty it was to intervene in domestic quarrels and attempt to reconcile man and wife. The society had disciplinary rules and expelled any of its members who were constant trouble-makers in the home. It took a prominent part as a group in Moslem festivals and staged formal receptions for co-religionists returning from the pilgrimage to Mecca. (Little, 1955*b*, p. 223.)

In the main, however, societies consisting entirely of women are concerned principally with trade and other economic matters. These organizations will be described in Chapter 7. In the meantime, it may be noted that various male associations also look after the occupational and professional interests of their members. For example, Busia has reported unions of carpenters, shoe-makers, drivers, seamen, sugar sellers, cooks, and stewards, etc., all of which also offered their members, as a principal benefit, the assurance of a decent burial (1950, p. 27). At Keta, according to Carey, the carpenters' union included all the hundred or so local practitioners of this trade. There was an *ad hoc* entrance fee, and each man gave as much as he felt he could afford. There were no fixed sickness benefits, but when a carpenter fell ill and went to hospital, the practice was for some of his colleagues, often including the chief-carpenter, to visit him and offer him the contents of their purse. If he died, wood was supplied by his family and made into a coffin for him by his colleagues free of charge. They also took a collection for the funeral expenses. In addition to the chief-carpenter, there was an executive committee of twelve, including a vice-president, a secretary, and a treasurer, which met three times a month to discuss matters of interest to the union. The secretary and the treasurer were literate and able to speak English, but the president's own lack of education often obliged him to use his educated son as a spokesman. (Carey.)

There are also modern crafts such as goldsmiths, tinkers, gunsmiths, tailors and barbers, as well as certain trade unions which, unlike Government-sponsored trade unions, have come spontaneously into being. One example of these was the Motor Drivers' Union at Keta which had become a branch of a nation-wide union negotiating freight rates, working conditions and so on. The Motor Drivers' Union differed from European trade unions in being an association of small entrepreneurs owning their own vehicles rather than an association of employees. It comprised transport owners as well as men employed as drivers and mates; the latter were associate members only. Membership was not compulsory, but in practice nearly all drivers joined. The main purpose was to look after the interests of drivers generally, and in particular to offer them legal assistance and insurance. When a driver was convicted, the Union tried as far as possible to pay his fine; and when a driver died the Union provided part of the funeral, sickness and accident benefits. (Carey.)

Finally, certain crafts have been incorporated into associations in ways which illustrate again the combination of modern functions and principles of organization with features deeply rooted in the traditional culture. For example, in traditional craft industries among the Yoruba, a father hands on his knowledge and skill to his sons, thus making some crafts the preserve of certain lineages. The sudden impact of Western technology did not give craftsmen an opportunity to adapt their work to the new machines and tools. New men were recruited who had never been craftsmen and so, when Lloyd studied these organizations in the early 1950's, the numerous tailors, carpenters, builders and their like were united to their fellow workers by bonds of economic agreement where their work was strictly regulated. The lineage no longer supplied the structure of the craft organization. It had been replaced by a system of guilds which strikingly resembled craft organizations in medieval Europe, and the lineage merely retained responsibility for the crafts practised before the advent of the European. (Lloyd, 1953, pp. 30–44.)

The initiative in forming a guild came from the workers themselves and not from kings or chiefs. One craftsman would visit his fellow workers, call a meeting of them, and rules and regulations were drafted. The first rule of all guilds was that every craftsman, whether master, journeyman, or apprentice, must register with the guild, must attend meetings, and must pay his dues. Failure to register could lead to confiscation of the offender's tools. There was a system for training apprentices who, unlike the traditional craftsmen, often worked away from home. The father or guardian of the boy would sign a contract with the master stating the length of the apprenticeship and the fee payable, the scale of premium usually being laid down by the guild. If the master was literate he might teach the boy, who was usually between the ages of fifteen and twenty, the rudiments of reading and writing in addition to the trade. All the work done by the boy belonged to the master and the apprentice received no remuneration for what he did. The guild member still retained full membership of his lineage and suffered no disabilities by joining another organization. Guild meetings were often occasions for conviviality; and members helped financially with each other's family ceremonies and celebrations. However, most forms of social security were still organized by the lineage, not by the guild. The latter did not undertake to care for its members in sickness or old age; nor did it function as a bank, lending money to members for tools. On the other hand, though it did not interest itself in disputes over a member's land or over his wives, the seduction of the wife of a fellow craftsman was condemned lest it cause enmity within the guild. (Lloyd, 1953, pp. 30–4.)

Recreation

Another special need catered for by urban associations is entertainment. Some of the groups concerned have developed out of the tribal societies and have retained a traditional character, including recruitment by age. For example, Ewe drumming companies active in Ghana towns are normally organized on a ward basis, there being three companies in every ward. The first comprises children; the second 'young men'; and the third, 'elders', i.e., the male population over the age of thirty or so. Actually, both men and women belong to drumming companies; but the leaders are always men and the women confine themselves to dancing and singing. At times, all three companies of a ward co-operate, but more often only one is used for any particular occasion. When an old man dies, for example, only the senior company will drum, while the middle company is primarily concerned with the funeral of a young man, and so on. If the dead man has been a leader of a drumming company a special collection is held towards his funeral expenses, but in the ordinary way company members only contribute by virtue of their membership of the ward. (Carey.)

As a rule these drumming companies will confine their activities to their own ward. However, when studied some ten years ago, they competed with each other for public appreciation and those with special skill became well known and might be employed by outsiders on special occasions. The result was that a few very well known companies were no longer recruited on a ward basis, but accepted only highly skilled and experienced drummers for membership. While their 'traditional' functions were to some extent retained, the companies at that stage resembled voluntary associations of semi-professional entertainers who travelled about the country in search of engagements. (Carey.)

Drum clubs cross-cut the entire age structure, but more Westernized forms of entertainment are supplied exclusively by young people. The dancing *compins* of Sierra Leone, characterized by Banton as young men's companies, are of the latter kind. As described below, they developed modern objectives and a more complex organization than the simple Mandinka dancing societies which gave them birth. Also, their dancing, as well as the music, shows strong signs of European influence and is somewhat reminiscent of English country dancing.

It starts with a line of four men and four women circling the floor to a slow tempo. A whistle is then blown and the men and women separate so that they dance opposite one another, several yards apart. In the next phase, they dance up to one another; right hand to right, left to left, backing and advancing; then they change places and repeat this much in the

way of English square-dancing—indeed the dance of one
company markedly resembles 'The Lancers'. After more
whistle blasts, any persons present may come on the floor,
where they dance together in mixed couples in what is said to
be a ballroom fashion and to a much faster tempo. This is an
obvious departure from traditional dancing. The dancers are
given items of clothing by their admirers in the audience and
these are worn on the head or over the shoulders for the rest
of the dance. Members of the audience also enter the ring to
place coins between the lips of the dancers, who, in turn,
allow the money to drop from their mouth on to a plate
carried round for this purpose by one of the company's
officials. This is a form of conspicuous consumption as well as
a method of donating money to the society. Women spectators
may also rise to wipe the sweat from the faces of male dancers
whom they particularly like. Most of the songs the women sing
are in honour of the company itself, of its founder, and praise
songs are also sung in order to honour some local notability or
to persuade rich onlookers to contribute funds.[1] (Banton,
pp. 172-6.) Such a 'play' is generally given in connection
with some important event, like the close of Ramadan or as

---

[1] Some examples quoted by Banton are as follows:

'Our play has been established: come and tell our people.
Ah! Come and tell our people in the Temne tribe.
Alimania! Come and tell our people in the Temne tribe.'

'Mammy Queen is an aristocrat!
Whatever she does is becoming to her.
Mammy Queen lives in Kissy Road:
It's her they're singing about.
Ai Turay, Oh, God bless him!'

'Alhaji Sisay has done well for us, God bless him!
Oh, good friendship is a (precious) thing.
Alhaji Sisay of the Temne tribe, when no one knew the Temne would
    progress:
Alhaji Sisay did well for us, God bless him!' (p. 174).

part of the ceremonies celebrating a wedding or a funeral. Money is also collected in weekly subscriptions from members.

In one of these organizations, which are particularly numerous among Temne and Mandinka immigrants in Freetown, this amount goes into a general fund to cover corporate expenses of the society's activities—rent of yard, provision of lamps, replacement of drum skins, etc. Then, when any member is bereaved, a collection is held to which all must contribute. However, quite an elaborate procedure is necessary before the money can be paid. The bereaved person must first notify the Reporter with a reporting fee. This is passed on to the company's Doctor, who investigates the circumstances of death, for the company will fine any member who has not notified them of a relative's illness so that they can see that the sick person receives attention. The Doctor washes the body and sends the Prevoe (Provost) round to the other members, telling them to gather that evening when they must pay their contributions. When anyone avoids payment without good cause, the Bailiff may seize an item of his property of equal value. The evening's meeting is organized by the Manager. He will bring the company's lamps, for members are under an obligation to take part in a wake which will last into the early hours. At the wake the bereaved person will provide cigarettes, kola-nuts, bread, and coffee, and will employ a singer. Another duty of the Doctor is to examine members before admission, and to attend them if sick. The Commissioner or Inspector is the disciplinary officer and he can arrest or eject trouble-makers, the Prevoe acting on his orders. The Clerk or Secretary keeps accounts and writes letters, and the Cashier receives from the Sultan for safe keeping any money accruing to the society. The Sultan is the chief executive; his female counterpart, who has charge of the women members, is the Mammy Queen. For the dancing, there is a leader who directs it, and a Conductor who supervises the band. There is also a Sister in charge of the Nurses, young girls who bring round refreshments at dances, often in white dresses with a red cross on the breast and the appropriate head gear. If there is no woman Doctor, an older Nurse or Sister may assist the Doctor with the invalids, or the washing of the corpse. There may also be further officials, such as an Overseer, an M.C., a Solicitor, a Lawyer, Sick Visitor, etc. Many of these titles involve no work, but they can be given to honour even the least deserving member and to strengthen his identification with the group's company. (Banton, pp. 171–2.)

Somewhat comparable societies of semi-professional entertainers performing traditional music on a commercial basis exist in other places. There were a dozen such groups in Brazzaville. They styled themselves Étoile Jeunesse, Opérette-Brazza, etc., and organized dances, played drums, or sang on festive occasions. The public was charged for admission and the receipts were divided among the performers according to seniority in the society, the president being entitled to four times as much as an ordinary member. Anything left over went towards the cost of new instruments and of further conviviality. One of these associations, consisting mainly of young artisans, had an older man—a fisherman—as their leader. They held their meetings in his compound and specialized in the singing of tribal songs. (Balandier, 1955b, pp. 143–4.)

Another organization in whose activities dancing and music play a prominent part is La Goumbé. This association virtually restricts membership to younger people and although the age limit on men is less rigid, only girls of marriageable age are admitted. La Goumbé, which is strongly represented in Abidjan, has many branches in the Ivory Coast and takes its name from a very popular dance resembling the beguine. Each branch has its own small orchestra which provides popular entertainment, including a satirical commentary on public affairs. What is even more interesting is the extent to which La Goumbé has taken over many of the old tribal functions while encouraging its members at the same time to preserve traditional ways. For example, it arranges the circumcision rites of their sons and marriages are contracted and celebrated under its auspices, including the provision of wedding presents and maternity benefits. In addition, as will be explained later, La Goumbé concerns itself with national politics, including acting as the local propaganda agent of Rassemblement Démocratique Africain. (Holas, 1953, pp. 116–31.)

Other groups concerned with entertainment—many of them organized by women—are very much smaller and quite informal. They may consist of six to a dozen persons who are kinsfolk, neighbours, and friends on intimate terms with each other. These persons meet in each other's houses or sit in the compound outside, organize convivial gatherings, and support each other at funerals, weddings, baptisms, etc., as well as saving up as a group for outings in other towns. The women concerned invariably turn out wearing the same style of dress and accessories in terms of smock, lappa, head-tie, sandals, necklace, etc. This custom is widely known by its Yoruba name—aso-ebi. Most of these activities take place after cocoa or some other cash crop has been harvested, i.e., at the time of the year when there is most money about; at the conclusion of Ramadan, or at Christmas. On these occasions, at a party or at any other kind of suitable social gathering the members may hire drummers and dance outside the house of the host, who is expected to give them money. They may also visit each other's relatives for similar purposes, receiving small 'dashes' from the people of the compound. In Sierra Leone, many of these dancing groups have 'devils'— a male masked performer who wears a black mask and a plentiful covering of straw. Although primarily for amusement and entertainment they frequently include some minor form of economic benefit. (Gamble; Baker; Banton, p. 187.)

4

MODERN ASSOCIATIONS

'Christian' Societies

FOR the most part, the associations described in the previous pages derive from traditional groupings and practices. They developed various Western procedures and have been adapted to modern purposes, but their mainspring is indigenous. They have been founded on and inspired by African ideas of co-operation.

There remains, however, the movement of modern associations which has a different origin. It derives not from Africa, but from the associational practices introduced originally by European administrators and missionaries. The principal objectives were usually defined in terms of advancing Christian practice or promoting education. That these ideas continue to be the main basis of common interest is not surprising in view of the subsequent rate of Westernization. In some of the coastal towns, adherents of Christian churches now comprise up to one-third of the population and the proportion of adult people who have attended school is increasing very rapidly.[1]

Among these 'modern' associations societies which are branches of a Christian church or which include the teaching and propagation of Christianity explicitly within their aims

---

[1] In Accra, for example, there were in 1955 some 40,000 adherents of the Mission churches, and some 4,360 adherents of the independent churches in a population of some 136,000, excluding new wards in the suburban area. A total of 86 per cent of all boys and girls of elementary school-going age attended elementary schools. (Acquah, pp. 145–7.)

comprise a distinct group. Religious practice is an integral part of the society's activity; meetings are generally conducted with prayers and hymns, and some instruction in Christianity may be given before the general business of the day is begun. Furthermore, whereas the 'traditional' societies rarely concern themselves with a member's religion, the 'Christian' associations either restrict their membership to persons who already profess Christianity or require people who join as non-Christians to undergo conversion and enrol themselves as members of a church within a given period of time. Also, although the latter groups have their mutual benefit schemes, they naturally lay more stress on securing the welfare of their members by spiritual means.

These church associations comprise a host of organizations catering for children as well as adult men and women, including women's fellowships and guilds, choirs, bible classes, boys' and girls' life brigades, boy scouts, girl guides, wolf cubs, brownies, etc. Many of them have specifically religious names such as Children of Mary, Apostleship of Prayer, Guild of the Good Shepherd, Sacred Heart, etc. Some require particular qualifications, such as Church marriage, but others open their doors more widely because, needless to say, not all Christian adherents are parties to a monogamous marriage, and organizations which exclude such persons would have few members. A Bible class of the Presbyterian Church in south-eastern Ghana, for example, is open to all baptized women of the congregation. Applications for membership are through the leader of the group who later introduces the applicant to the class. The officers, who are elected by the whole class, include the President or the Class Leader, Class Secretary, and Class Treasurer.[1] All officers are literate and full communicants

[1] Very often, these Bible classes acquire a special identity through being under the leadership of a particular teacher (Bandoh).

of the church. Of the rank and file, full communicants—literate or illiterate—may qualify for a badge, a crest of merit. (Fiawoo, 1959a, p. 91.) The business affairs and meetings of church associations of this kind are conducted in much the same way as a secular club.

Two associations in Kumasi will briefly illustrate their usual services to their own members and the wider community. The Scapular Confraternity is one of several societies organized within the Roman Catholic Church. Membership is open only to men, but there is no age limit. It was founded more than 30 years ago and in addition to helping its members both spiritually and financially in times of sickness and at death, it tries to assist in other ways when the need is urgent. For example, when a widower with two children died outside the reach of any of his own relatives, the society paid his hospital expenses and gave him a decent burial; the children were adopted by a member, the Catholic Mission paying for the education. The general rule, however, is for prayers to be said at Mass for a member who is ill, and he is given a small amount of money until he is well. If he dies, the society pays for a special Mass for the soul of the deceased member by providing candles for the church. No financial aid, however, is given to his relatives, the society being merely concerned with the spiritual welfare of its members in this regard. (Bandoh.)

The Methodist Women's Fellowship is a branch of the 'Mother Fellowship' of the church in Accra and it serves in turn as a 'Mother Fellowship' for the towns and villages in Ashanti where this particular set of church groups has been established. The Fellowship organizes special classes for religious education, and its members are recruited for evangelical work and sent out preaching on Sunday afternoon in prisons, hospitals, and other institutions as well as in the suburbs of Kumasi. The 'missionaries' concerned report back to a general meeting of the society, where a discussion of their results and difficulties is led by the minister of the church. Groups of members are also sent out on charitable visits during the week to people who are sick or blind or are in other kinds of trouble, the gifts being voluntarily provided. In addition, the society arranges for its members to receive instruction, free of charge, in such things as housecraft, child care, knitting and other useful hobbies. Members of the society who teach give their services voluntarily, but non-members are offered a small honorarium for their trouble. There are the usual sickness and other benefit schemes. (Bandoh.)

The above societies are associated of course with the orthodox churches, but the numerous 'independent' churches are equally fertile in the development of associations. For example, there is the Apostolic Revelation Society in south-eastern Ghana whose members almost exclusively inhabit a particular ward of the town and lead a communal life centred on the Prophet-founder. They run a clinic and a school which are, in principle, open to members and non-members alike. This society also has its own farms, raising food crops and animals. (Fiawoo, 1959a, pp. 93-4.)

Among the many church societies catering for women, there are usually a series of groups. These range from the wives of church dignitaries, full members of the church, to women who may be the wives of polygynists and illiterate, although members of the congregation. As in the church congregations themselves women appear greatly to predominate. Thus according to figures supplied by Acquah concerning mid-week activities of the Accra churches in 1955, some 6,051 persons, including 3,771 women and 1,960 men, took part in societies associated with overseas Mission churches and some 1,600 persons, including 951 women and 614 men, in societies associated with independent African churches. (Acquah, pp. 292–3.)

Women's groups have also played a large part in the development of church life in southern Nigeria. In some congregations, these unions and fellowships tend to follow the *egbe* pattern; there being separate *egbe* for men and for women of comparable age or marital status. (Lloyd, 1959, p. 53.) In other congregations they are modelled on classes, i.e., they are presided over by one dominant woman—the wife of a clergyman or of a teacher—and the other women attend to learn the Bible or to discuss ways of raising money. These rank and file members also carry out much of the material work of the church, such as decorating it, making altar cloths, etc. In most churches, too, there are policy-making women of higher status who meet in the house of the bishop's wife and talk over matters of general importance. Women in this position are sought after by the church associations, and are frequently invited to become patroness of a particular group. The result is that the composition and organization of church societies in Nigeria is somewhat variable. In the Anglican church and in many of the independent churches, for example, the women's groups are largely composed of matrons or of women past the first years of marriage and child bearing. Younger women are slower to join, possibly because they have less time to spare from family responsibilities. Yet, paradoxically, the Roman Catholics and the Baptists are able to get groups of girls, mostly school children, together in western Nigeria, but find the older women more difficult to organize. The Baptist churches have a highly disciplined series of groups which are ranked in stages according to age. Each stage has a name, e.g., Sunbeam, Ladies in Waiting, etc., and each such group is expected to perform particular duties as well as to acquire some knowledge of the Bible and of Baptist church history. Older girls and women are trained as leaders for these groups and as home visitors. (Baker.)

These Nigerian societies not only exert a certain pressure on their members, but try through them to influence the husbands and the children. Some of them, for example, invite the husbands of members to meetings in order to discuss the difficulties of modern marriage—a problem which to the women (see Chapter 7) often seems insoluble. Guidance is also given individually in some cases. In Lagos, the women who take the lead in these and other matters are generally the wives of church officials, and Mission-trained teachers; in the provincial towns it is generally the modern élite. Sometimes, in addition to weekly meetings and services, church societies have special celebrations like annual harvests, picnics and excursions which are very popular. Functions within the church include stage cantatas and Nativity plays. They also hold parades, headed by a brass band, as a means of advertising their activities and attracting fresh recruits. So much money is expended in preparation for these outings, particularly on clothes, that one of the most popular criticisms advanced against the churches in Ghana (and probably elsewhere) is that they encourage extravagance by setting the stage for competitive dress display, especially by the women. (Busia, 1950, p. 78.)

In addition to the above societies, many associations are concerned to promote Christian ideals without being specifically attached or affiliated to a church body. Some of them include traditional methods of mutual aid within their organization; others are organized almost wholly on modern lines. Two of the best known and most widely spread of the latter are inter-denominational—the Young Men's Christian Association and the Young Women's Christian Association.

The YWCA has a long history of work in Nigeria, although

its fortunes have fluctuated since its earlier days when it had the support of wives of European officials and did pioneering work in Lagos and Onitsha in setting up domestic science schools for girls. It housed the girls, and provided a two-year course in hygiene, sewing and baby craft for which there was a certificate of proficiency. These schools were popular, and Africans in government service encouraged their fiancées and young wives to attend them. The YWCA also ran girls' clubs in Lagos and one or two other towns, and it has interested itself in boarding houses for girls attending secondary schools or working in offices in places away from their home town. These girls frequently lodge with friends and relatives, but there is an increasing number of girls who cannot be looked after in this way, who take rooms in strange houses, share accommodation with other girls, and live under unsatisfactory conditions. The YWCA would like to establish 'Fellowship groups' in every large town for the use of these people. Some YWCA hostels and community centres do exist, but there are certain difficulties. One is that younger educated girls are not popular among many of the middle-aged women whose support is indispensable if any voluntary work or fund raising is to be carried out. They resent the attraction of these younger women for their husbands and so the most successful groups seem to be those which cater for older women. (Baker.)

There is also a branch of the YWCA at Accra which in 1956 had some 130 members, including adults and teen-agers. Its activities include religious study, lectures, drama, outdoor and indoor games, demonstrations in cookery, arts and crafts, excursions and socials. Apparently, there are three separate kinds of membership and the programme of activities is arranged according to literacy, illiteracy and age. This, as in many of the traditionally based associations, creates a large number of offices and results directly or indirectly in nearly everyone sharing some of the responsibility. There is also the Young Men's Christian Association which is a much larger group, catering for about 600 members. Omitting cookery, its activities were much the same as the YWCA, but included boxing, physical training, and photography in addition. (Acquah, p. 316.) A much smaller branch of the YMCA at Takoradi had 80 members in 1950 (Busia, 1950, p. 79).

A few undenominational societies of local origin also enjoy wide support over the Akan area and some places outside. These are the 'Hope Society' and the 'Honesty Society' which at Takoradi have respectively 888 and 500 members. Each of these societies has a junior and a senior membership and it is open to both sexes, literates and illiterates alike. Distinctive uniforms are worn at meetings. The prime function of these associations is to provide their members, when deceased, with a decent burial. Like the church societies, their social activities include annual picnics and church parades, and they also have prayers, scripture readings and hymns. (Busia, 1950; Clarkson.)

In Kumasi, a number of the benevolent societies have a specifically philanthropic function. These organizations are the successors of fraternities which in the earlier years of the century were popularly known as English and American lodges; they were labelled with such names as 'The Band of Hope', and most of their members had embraced Christianity. The aim of these present-day societies is the pursuit of goodness through acts of charity and kindness. Members are taught that the worldly acquisition of material goods is harmful to spiritual development unless a person is willing to share his blessings with others, especially the poor, the needy, and the handicapped. These societies are not primarily concerned with assisting their own members, and although financial aid is given in times of sickness and death and in an emergency, it is regarded as 'special aid'—a very different attitude from that of other societies. Membership is open to adults of both sexes, irrespective of religious affiliation and of ethnic group. The name of these associations, *Bedan—agya kuo* ('Everything will be left behind'), symbolizes the guiding principles of its activities which include the making from time to time of charitable bequests to public institutions, such as Blind and Leper settlements, hospitals, and mental asylums. (Bandoh.)

'Cultural' Associations

Mention has already been made of the influence of education in promoting these 'modern' associations. In general, their aim is to foster the moral or intellectual progress of their members. The 'Christian' societies, therefore, have their counterpart in organizations which have cultural or social objectives. Both categories of association are explicitly Western in orientation, but the cultural associations usually recruit their membership at a more advanced level of education. Their main *raison d'etre*, and the common bond of interest, is specifically in the attainment of modern cultural and social standards.

In some cases this cultural distinction is formally recognized by confining membership exclusively to people marked out by a certain degree of 'civilization', education or 'advancement'. Thus, the conditions of admission into the Association of the Évolués of Stanleyville limit membership to those who (a) hold a diploma of post-primary studies; (b) practise a respectable calling similar to that of holders of a diploma under (a); (c) follow a respectable trade, and are distinguished by their knowledge and professional pride; (d) stand out among their fellows in behaviour and general morals. This regulation goes on: 'Apart from fulfilling the above conditions, the candidate must be either monogamously married, or a single man of good reputation. Polygamy and even bigamy, as well as any

74

dishonourable sentence exclude him automatically. Nevertheless, those who have atoned for their faults by some years of
blameless life may be admitted.' The AES is composed of men,
but there is also the Association of Advanced Babua Women
which recruits members on the basis of both education and
tribal affiliation. (Clément, pp. 473–4.)

It appears that the Committee of the AES, after recruiting
at first almost exclusively among clerks, school teachers, and
male nurses, wished to make it possible for deserving manual
workers to join. In other words, they added 'respectable
behaviour' to the original criteria of education and work.
However, in some other associations—those formed by the
former pupils of certain schools—education is implicitly, at
any rate, an essential qualification.[1] One of the latter organizations is the Old Bo Boys Association, known colloquially as
OBBA. Bo School was originally started by the Government
of Sierra Leone for the education and training of the sons of
chiefs, and so a large number of OBBA members are paramount chiefs or belong to chiefs' families. Teachers on the staff
of Bo School are also allowed to join the Association. It holds
its annual meeting at the School, all the business being conducted in English. The two days' proceedings include a cricket
match against the School XI and are concluded by a gala dance
in the *barri* (court house) of the local Native Administration, to
which all the neighbouring notabilities, European as well as
African, are invited. Chiefs who are Old Boys come to this
function attended by their followers, and wear traditional dress.

Although the functions of this type of association are predominantly social—running football teams and holding peri-
odic reunions—they sometimes spread over into other fields.

[1] For example, although the statutes of a Stanleyville association stipulate
that membership shall be confined to former pupils of the school concerned,
they also make provision for the former pupils of other schools. The association
is thus open to all who are 'literate'. (Clément, p. 475.)

The Old Achimotan Association in the former Gold Coast, for example, in the period immediately following the Second World War, took the initiative in organizing and conducting classes for Kumasi workers. The Association des Anciens Elèves du Lycée Terrason de Fongerès at Bamako was instrumental in bringing into being the first trade union in the French Sudan in 1937. (Hodgkin, 1956, pp. 88–9.) Another association which developed wider aims was the Egbe Omo Oduduwa. Translated, this means the Society of the Descendants of Omo Oduduwa, who was the mythical founder of the Yoruba peoples. This society was originally organized in London, but it was re-founded in Nigeria in 1948 as a Yoruba cultural association. In addition to fostering study of the Yoruba language, culture and history; planning to provide secondary school and University scholarships for Yoruba boys and girls; and seeking to protect Yoruba monarchical institutions; it also propagated the idea of a Yoruba state within a Nigerian federal constitution. (Coleman, 1958, pp. 342–3.)

Other cultural societies founded by educated Africans often take the form of literary and debating clubs. These generally have an educational aim, such as helping people to improve their proficiency in the speaking of English. One example is the Unser-Ud-Dean Society which came into being in 1923 to carry out a plan for Moslem education. Later, it established branches in some of the larger centres. The Islamic Society of Nigeria was founded in 1924 in Lagos. (Smythe, p. 33.) In Ghana, there is the Peoples' Educational Association (P.E.A.) which, like the Workers' Educational Association in Britain, works in conjunction with the University Extra-Mural Department. It tries to stimulate intellectual life and an interest in such topics as current affairs and politics. (Carey.)

Although concerned with writing lectures, debating and book reviewing, these study circles, and other associations organized by the intelligentsia, in time included in their activities discussions of political and economic questions. Quite often they were founded by men who later became leading politicians. For example, Nnamdi Azikiwe, organized one of these societies—the Youngman's Literary Association—in 1923. A related development was the institution in Nigeria of branches of the West African Students' Union, which was set up in London in the 1920's, as a centre for the discussion of ideas and became the main political and social meeting place for Nigerian students in the United Kingdom for the next twenty years. (Coleman, 1958, pp. 204-7; Garigue.)

Africans as well as Europeans also belong to cultural societies sponsored by the British Council and by l'Alliance Française, the Council's French counter part. In 1956, the British Council's branch in Accra had 400 members, including some 160 females. In addition to a choral society there are drama groups, and members meet regularly for play reading and periodically stage plays for the general public. Other similar associations in Accra include film societies. (Acquah, p. 154.)

Much more widely popular, however, are the social clubs which are found in many of the smaller towns as well as in the main urban centres. In the countries formerly under British rule these institutions, however modest their premises and equipment, are modelled quite clearly on the 'European' clubs established by European officials. Facilities quite often include a hall with cushioned chairs, small tables, a bar, and a dance floor, sometimes with a games room of sorts, and perhaps an open terrace. Occasionally there is a tennis court and there may be a small library. The Bo African Club is fairly typical. This was started about 1942, and, prior to the founding of similar clubs in other small towns, was the main social centre for educated Africans in the Sierra Leone provinces. The great majority of its members are people who have been to school. Theoretically, membership is 'open to all', but the entrance fee and monthly subscription are usually beyond the means of people in more poorly paid jobs, and hence of most non-literate persons. Moreover, the kind of activity pursued there —talks, lectures, debates, etc.—excludes, or is unlikely to appeal to, a person who has not had a Western education. These proceedings, as well as all official business, are conducted in English. Nor are persons wearing native dress admitted into the weekly dance—one of the club's principal activities— the general custom being for women to wear a print or silk dress (without the head-tie), and men open-necked shirts with a sports jacket or blazer. On gala nights evening dress is worn by both sexes. (Little, 1955b, pp. 220–1.)

The principal offices are those of President, Vice-President, and General Secretary. There are also the Financial Secretary, the Society Secretary, who organizes dances and other forms of entertainment, the Literary Secretary, in charge of the club's small library and store of periodicals, and the Tialler. The Tialler notifies members about meetings, etc., and collects dues and subscriptions on behalf of the Financial Secretary. These posts are filled by election, but the presidential office is generally reserved for some popular individual relatively senior in government service. For example, two past presidents of the Bo African Club have been the Acting Principal of Bo School, and the Assistant Director of Medical Services. Both are Creoles, and it is significant, for reasons to be explained later, that Creole members in general take a leading part in the organization of this as well as other up-country clubs. In addition to its ordinary activities, the Bo African Club under-takes a number of public functions, including special dances to honour important visitors to the town. It also entertains the teams of visiting football clubs, and its premises are used for a variety of purposes including political meetings and adult education classes. Such occasions are open to the general public, and local notabilities—African and European—are often invited. The club also invites Europeans to tennis tournaments, and matches between African and European teams are played under its auspices. (Little, 1955b.)

In Accra, the total membership of clubs of this kind was some 3,000 in 1956 (Acquah pp. 160–2). In Nigeria, the best known is the Island Club of Lagos which is patronized very widely by the élite, including ministers of state, high ranking government officials, professional and business men. It holds cinema shows and dances and its membership, over more than 1,000, includes many people from overseas as well as from African countries, in addition to Nigeria.

There are also dining clubs which are more exclusive. In Accra, one is a men's club and the other is a women's club, and the members of these clubs dine together once a month, a guest speaker usually being invited. The men's dining club restricts its membership to twenty Africans and twenty Europeans; the women's dining club to fifteen Africans and fifteen Europeans. The Ladies' Dining Club in Lagos is similarly divided equally between the wives of European officials and Nigerian women. Husbands are occasionally, but rarely, invited as guests to its meetings which are held at the most expensive hotel in town. (Baker.) Both the senior and the junior branches of the civil service also have dining clubs. European and African women also meet socially in the Corona society. This association was originally confined to the wives of British officials, but it has now opened its doors to African women of comparable status. It helps its members to find accommodation in the United Kingdom, provides introductions, and finds assistance in looking after children on sea voyages.

Another species of social club for women are Ladies' Clubs and Women's Institutions, some of the latter being associated with church bodies. Since a large number of literate husbands have non-literate wives, some of these women's clubs reflect the sociological situation by being divided into 'literate' and 'illiterate' sections which hold separate meetings. 'Literate' activities consist mainly in sewing and crochet work, in practising the cooking of European and native dishes, and in listening to talks about household economy. Individual literate women give instruction in these arts at the 'illiterate' meeting and in return non-literate women teach the 'literate' group such things as garra-dyeing, basketry, spinning, and some of the traditional songs and dances. Sometimes money is collected for educational purposes. For example, a Women's Institute, under the auspices of the EUB Mission, hopes to provide one of its girls with a scholarship to a secondary school, its aim being 'to raise the standard of womanhood in Sierra Leone'. (Little, 1955b, pp. 221-2.) The Keta Women's Institute is another example. It was started by educated women; the president and the leading officers of this club are teachers, but the bulk of its membership consists of market women. Members meet twice monthly, and lecturers are invited from outside, in addition to local speakers. The subjects discussed usually deal with topics of special interest to women, including child-care, knitting, hygiene and so on. There are also regular classes in cookery and needle-work. (Carey.)

Women who are relatively wealthy and socially prominent are found more frequently in international organizations such as the Red Cross. The work of the latter's committees in Lagos is voluntary and consists mainly in raising funds for charitable purposes. This is done largely by patronage, by appealing for money to the larger business firms, and by running baby shows and bazaars. New members are attracted by the society's high social standing derived from the well-known names of its patrons and committee members, and this has enabled the Red Cross to start branches all over the western region of Nigeria. The procedure, when the time comes for an appeal to be made, is to place matters in the hands of a paid organizer, who is assisted by local members to raise money. Members hold committee meetings in each other's houses. (Baker.) The Red Cross is also strongly established in Ghana, where its Accra branch supplies a number of welfare and medical services. It arranges talks, discussions, debates, etc., as well as maintaining attendance at first-aid posts; first-aid work at public functions, meetings and sports gatherings; home visits to the aged and infirm; repatriation of patients to their home towns, etc. (Acquah, pp. 120, 136, 137.) Socially prominent women have also founded many charitable societies of their own, and quite often these organizations have developed into national federations.

So far as is known, masonic lodges and fraternities generally follow the European pattern, but among the exceptions is the Reformed Ogboni Fraternity. This is a combination of ideas borrowed from Freemasonry and the most important politically of the Yoruba cult groups: the Ogboni. Although originally conceived as a Christian society, the ROF is now open to non-Christians and, despite the opposition of Islam to secret societies, a number of Moslems have joined. Its leaders use traditional titles, and costumes are worked of coloured cloth, bearing the symbols of the society, such as three straight vertical lines, a triangle and two eyes. In each district, the head of the local society is called 'father of the occult'. Members call each other brother or 'son of the same mother'. Membership is said to be important if a person is in commerce or is concerned with politics. Those who belong to it are generally well-to-do and of the educated class. (Parrinder, pp. 178–80; Morton-Williams.) In a Lagos branch the subscription was 10s. a month, and the qualifications for membership included integrity, punctuality, and a degree of seniority. The Society would help to find work for members, particularly in Government service, and assist them in difficulties. (Marris, p. 42.)

Finally, sports clubs are a further important form of Western activity. Football (soccer) is particularly popular in the coastal regions and there are numerous clubs in every large town, including persons of every class. These are generally organized in leagues, and matches between the better known teams attract a gate of several thousands and are reported at length in the daily newspapers. There are inter-town and inter-province matches, and matches are also played between teams representing the various West African countries and against visiting teams of professional players from Europe. A number of the African teams concerned have European trainers and some of the others are helped at times by European army officers and police officers. (Acquah, pp. 155–6.)

Cricket is confined to the English-speaking countries and is played mainly by young men who have been to school. It is not so highly organized as football, although regular matches are played between teams representing their countries. Other games such as lawn tennis, hockey, and table tennis, are played for the most part within a more comprehensive club or centre, including various social clubs. There are also a number of boxing clubs and athletic groups and associations, as well as a few golf clubs and polo clubs catering for the well-to-do, both African and European. Finally, race meetings are held in a number of places, including Accra. The Race Course there is owned by the Accra Turf Club which was founded in 1924. Membership of it is limited to 150 members, all of whom are males; in 1956 eight of these were Africans. Race meetings are attended by about 4,000 people and there are always at least 100 horses competing which are owned by Africans, Europeans and Lebanese. (Acquah, pp. 155–7)

Part Two

5

THE MIGRANT AND THE URBAN COMMUNITY

I SUGGESTED earlier that African social change and transformation might be seen as an historical process of adaptation to new conditions of life and labour. These new conditions originate basically in something extraneous to West Africa itself, namely the industrial economy of the West. This market economy, along with other factors of Western contact, has extended the local scale of relationships and has brought indigenous societies into a wider social system than that of the tribe or even the nation. It also involves a greater specialization of institutions, thereby giving rise to a larger variety of new social groupings and networks than in the traditional system. At the same time, there is cultural and social continuity, because much of the older way of life persists despite migration and other factors.

In this context, therefore, adaptation proceeds through modification of the traditional institutions and their combination with Western cultural values, technology, and economic practices into a new social structure. The fresh functional relations involved are made possible by the restructuring of traditional roles and by the development of roles derived from the encompassing industrial system.

Voluntary associations assist this adaptive process by providing a new basis for social organization, which is all the more important because of the industrial town's lack of integration in comparison with the rural areas. Accra, for example, contains the representatives of more than sixty-five different tribes and peoples, and the populations of other large urban centres is hardly less varied. Even in the smaller towns with less than 15,000 inhabitants there are frequently the elements of at least a dozen different tribes. The presence of educated Africans as well as Europeans and Asians adds further to the cultural mosaic and has to be taken into account, quite apart from age-old enmities and alliances between the tribes themselves. One of the most obvious in Ghana is the hostility of the Zabramas and the Gaos against the Hausas, and the friendship between the Moshies and the Zabramas; the Fulani are not popular with any group. These groups regard themselves as Moslems, but Islam is not strong enough on its own to override these differences and so the migrants have only one thing in common: they are foreigners. As such they are shunned by the indigenous inhabitants for whom any migrant is straight away assimilated with the natives of the Northern Territories: he is a 'bushman', a naked barbarian. The migrants retort in similar terms and refer to the people of the Coast as 'sons of slaves'.[1] (Rouch, pp. 59, 62.)

Divided thus by traditional attitudes as well as by language, custom and religion the town can have no single system of social norms. Over inheritance, over marriage, and over many other institutions essential to community life notions of law and justice differ and there are no common bases for

[1] Similar attitudes have been noted in Freetown where, until fairly recently, the term usually applied to a tribal migrant was 'aborigine'. About the northern migrants' reaction in Ghana, Rouch adds the following: 'The Zabrama ... confident in his ancient civilization, regards the Coast man, whether in a dickey or a Jaguar, as a "Gurunsi", a descendent of the slaves whom Babatu used to exchange for a kola-nut in the market.... This proud attitude of the least "kaya kaya" in rags toward the lawyer or doctor who brushes him in his car is one of the most extraordinary facets of behaviour it is possible to see in the Gold Coast' (p. 60).

agreement. Nor can the town's own civic institutions give the lead when for most of the migrants the place in which they do their business is not a permanent home. They may own property, may make repeated visits, spend part of the year there, but without acquiring any feelings of attachment. Their social self remains in some other part of the country— among their lineage people in the place where they were born. Also, as we shall see later, owing to the clash of modern with traditional ideas of marriage family institutions are under a special strain. And there is increased tension in relations between the sexes and between different generations.

In these terms the industrialized town presents a picture of conflicting as well as changing standards. It implies a social and psychological situation which might amount to Durkheim's notion of anomie were it not that voluntary associations provide a link between the traditional and the urban way of life. The new cults are an obvious example because in them indigenous beliefs are syncretized with supposedly more up-to-date forms of religion—Christianity and Islam. But ethnic unions and other such organizations similarly blend apparently divergent aims and interests. On the one hand, they emphasize tribal duties and obligations; on the other, they urge the adoption of a modern outlook and they establish new social practices. What is significant about this duality is that by continuing such familiar norms as kinship, the provision of proper burial rites, etc., the associations make the innovations seem less strange. They build for a migrant a cultural bridge and in so doing they convey him from one kind of social universe to another.

This is the case because, as their characteristic activities and objectives show, voluntary associations serve many of the same needs as the kin group and the lineage. Fraternity, for example, is particularly stressed; so much so that members are expected actively to regard each other as brothers and sisters, to sympathize with each other in time of difficulty, visiting each other when sick, and swelling the procession at a funeral. Sociability is also encouraged by the general practice of serving refreshments at every formal gathering of members —usually held at fortnightly or monthly intervals. Periodical outings, picnics and excursions, and more convivial gatherings such as dances, foster the same feeling. And social solidarity is further enhanced by emblems, mottoes and banners and by the custom of wearing a uniform style of dress. These regular meetings make for stability in the migrant's contacts because, as the figures above will have shown, a large proportion of the urban population is transient—people continuously come and go. Also, they help to restore to him the sense of identity he may have lost in moving so far away from his own community. Since one of the migrant's main needs is to be regarded as a person it is significant that many associations have a host of minor titles and offices available, thereby giving even the most humble member an opportunity to feel that he 'matters'.

Closely related to the latter problem is that of the migrant's general re-orientation. This is obviously important because when the individual who is not content to remain in his rural village reaches the city, he learns that many of the traditional bonds are no longer available to him. He is no longer in a close-knit, tightly organized community and the sudden release from old ways and values leaves a vacuum which can be filled by new and different ones. In particular, having entered into an economic system founded on wages and profits, he needs versatility for dealing with the problems of getting a living, and he needs to adjust himself to an extended and unrestricted field of social relationships due to the multiplicity of contacts with 'foreigners'. (Balandier, 1956.)

One of the ways in which associations aid the migrant's

adaptation in these respects is by providing him with information about what is going on in the town. It will probably be some time before he adjusts to the idea of urban life being controlled not by individuals but by organizations, government departments, business firms, etc. An association keeps him in touch not only with his own people at home but with the town's institutions. It serves as a go-between if, for example, he needs an interpreter, and it introduces him to useful contacts, such as employers of labour, headmen of gangs, officials at the Employment Exchange, etc. The association also reduces the migrant's isolation by acting as a 'civilizing' agency on his behalf. (Fiawoo, 1959a, p. 92.) It inculcates new standards of dress, social behaviour and personal hygiene; the advantage from the migrant's point of view being that he is regarded no longer as a 'country bumpkin' but is able to keep pace with his new neighbours. The association's own administration is a further means whereby he can achieve a more sophisticated status, because by taking on a particular duty, however minor, the migrant learns a fresh role. He is generally encouraged to branch out in this way and the fact that many of the office-holders concerned have Western titles, such as Doctor and Nurse, is not necessarily make-believe. It may signify the deliberate assumption of an already known and attractive pattern of conduct which the members concerned desire to follow. (Banton, p. 182.)

What the migrant learns is also very helpful to him in practical terms. There are, for example, the association's rules, including fines for late attendance at meetings, which teach useful habits of punctuality. Thrift is encouraged by the demand for regular payment of dues, and its practice is taught by mutual benefit schemes as well as by the savings clubs themselves. Presumably the lesson is well dinned home because the part played by these contribution clubs and similar practices in the acquisition of goods—produce for trading, a bicycle, etc.—and in bride-wealth is considerable.[1] It is said that a man does not work in order to save money: he rather works in order to obtain his 'take-out' to pay for what he wants. (Ardener, 1953, pp. 139–40.) Also, not only do these schemes help to supply the migrant with ready cash, but they take elaborate precautions—thumb-printing, counter-signing, etc.—against fraud. They teach him, in fact, how to keep an account of cash and the safest way in which to conduct his own business dealings. More specifically, associations concerned with a particular trade accept initiates for training. A younger member has the opportunity of apprenticing himself in this way and of learning from watching or talking to the older and more experienced members. He may also acquire a smattering of literacy through the association's more formal efforts at education. Since many of the societies also teach modern hobbies and crafts, women have the same opportunities, including the earning of pocket-money for themselves. Crochet-work, in particular, seems to be a profitable side-line.

Finally, associations which have a tribally mixed membership enable the migrant to meet on friendly terms people of different origin. By assigning to him some common task in the society's activities they accustom him to the idea of co-operation with strangers. They help the migrant in this way to add to his stock of languages and to get better used to the kind of cosmopolitan atmosphere which he has to adapt himself to in the world outside. Nor do they necessarily circumscribe his choice of friends and acquaintances because quite often there is a system

[1] Tribal unions have their own savings schemes, but among workers on a Cameroons plantation contribution clubs were by far the most important means of saving. Not only were they the most common, but average contributions to them were much higher than to other forms of investment. (Warmington and Ardener, p. 178.)

of affiliation offering reciprocal privileges of membership between different branches of the same group of associations.

In addition to moral and material support, voluntary associations also substitute for the kin group in providing for a good deal of the migrant's protection. This is the case because nowadays it is to the head of an association rather than to his lineage that a person in trouble turns for help or advice. He consults first the secretary or the president of, say, his tribal union. The latter refers the matter to the committee, and if it is a question of money the case is probably put before the entire association at its next meeting. Decisions involving the expenditure of cash are rarely taken without the consent of all the members and, in some cases, the society's money cannot be disbursed without a written order containing the principal officials' signatures. Alternatively, the person in difficulty may approach one of the society's patrons. The patrons are generally individuals of high social standing, such as a chief, a barrister, etc. They have been appointed on account of their local influence and in the expectation that they will use it on the society's behalf. If this appeal fails, it is quite common for the association itself to back a deserving member by paying for his legal expenses in the event of the case going to court. To be able to count on this assistance and the active support of fellow members is the more necessary because, unlike his situation at home, the migrant is frequently housed among strangers. In Accra, for example, Acquah found that more than four out of every five households shared dwellings with other families (pp. 49–50), and in Freetown families from four or five different tribes sometimes share the same house.[1]

Voluntary associations also help to protect their member's occupational interests. Women traders, for example, boycott fellow-traders who under-cut prices and among the new

[1] Personal communication.

guilds described above wage rates are fixed according to the type of work done. This enables the craftsmen concerned to maintain a set level but no objection is raised to their charging friends and relatives less; nor does the guild mind if a rich customer can be persuaded to pay a higher rate. At the same time, the guild tries to maintain a reasonable standard of work in the craft and protects the customer against the craftsman who receives an advance payment for his work and then fails, without good reason, to complete the contract and is unable to refund the money. It also stops members from stealing work from each other. If a guild member is accused by some person outside the guild, and, in the opinion of the guild, the charges are unfounded, the guild will intercede on his behalf and the members' contribution will be used to fight the case in the King's Court. In judging cases between its own members the guild orders one or both parties to the dispute to pay a fine which will be used to buy beer for consumption at the meeting. There is a heavier fine if disrespect is shown to the guild head. The latter may be the eldest man practising the craft; or the first man to practise in that particular town; or he may be elected by the members and have neither of these qualifications. (Lloyd.)

Equally important—not only to the migrants, but to most of the urban population in general—is the question of supernatural protection. This kinship function, too, has been largely taken over by voluntary associations. The main reason is that individual and social problems in the urban environment are apparently beyond the scope of traditional ritual. There are, for example, acts of physical violence, robbery and petty larceny, drunkenness and prostitution. (Busia, 1950, pp. 84–114.) There are also various illnesses, such as venereal disease, which cause sterility and melancholia as well as physical discomfort. These new malaises and disorders of society are very much more common in the town than in the countryside, and so the tendency, quite often, is to assume that they are the result of witchcraft and other evil influences. Somewhat similarly, the competitive spirit evoked by new occupations is rationalized in terms of personal fortune or misfortune having a supernatural connection. A farmer growing cocoa for cash, for example, may lose his entire crop through blight, or a clerk may be dismissed from his post in an office. The explanation—malevolent forces are at work; jealous rivals possess a medicine more powerful than one's own.[1]

For difficulties of the above kind the indigenous religion is too generalized in its methods to offer a solution. It has a remedy for everyday mishaps and it purports to ward off the calamities—failure of crops, depredations by wild animals, sudden storms and floodings—which ordinarily endanger the life and health of rural people. For the new worries and anxieties of the townsman it has no real answer. In contrast, the syncretist cults and sects give greater assurance and are more specific. Not only do they profess to cure both supernaturally and naturally caused disease and offer prophylactic protection against evil forces in general, they also claim the ability to detect and root out witches. They cater also for the special hazards and needs of urban life—accidents caused by motor transport, school, and professional examinations, interviews for a job, success in lovemaking, consolation in marriage, fame in outdoor sport, etc. By strictly forbidding their members to make use of sorcery and bad magic they alleviate mistrust and engender greater confidence in social relationships. The following testimony of a cult priest in eastern Ghana explains the underlying psychology:

[1] Compare M. J. Field, pp. 175–6.

Several years ago I served as leader of a drum party an Anloga. Our main objectives were mutual-aid, fun and recreation. In the bid to outshine one other party in the community, we soon became bitter rivals. Our drum parties degenerated into *Halowu* (i.e. antagonistic drum parties). Each party composed songs full of the harshest epithets and invectives against members of the other. So strained were our relations that we had no qualms in using charms against each other. As leader of my party, I felt it my duty to protect the interests of my group. Naturally, I had recourse to all the protective charms I could come by; but these were not always efficacious, since a powerful charm easily succumbed to a more powerful one. Our drum parties were, in course of time, disbanded on orders of the chiefs who could not bear the seeds of rancour we were sowing in the community. This did not ease the situation, for we remained in mortal fear of each other. It was at the height of this despair that I learnt of Blekete as a prophylaxis against all 'magical' influences. But I had not the faintest idea what were the rules of membership. I travelled to Asanyra (in Fantiland) where I 'ate the medicine'. It worked. I felt quite at ease with a real peace of mind I never had before. Much later, the idea dawned on me that I might be releasing the fears of my friends if I helped to bring the cult within their reach. This was the original motive that led me to Kpoglu for my long apprenticeship. [Fiawoo, 1959*b*]

Nor are the syncretist cults and messianic movements alone in performing these functions. Among the Moslem groups, too, there are many similar practices, including the provision of charms and the manufacture of talismans and other magical devices. Christianity, in addition, has a similar popular reputation—mainly through its association with the superior technology of Europeans. As a result, participation in Christian rituals is thought by many illiterate members of church associations to afford more effective forms of supernatural protection than they can obtain elsewhere. Women, in particular, believe that it will ward off or remove the curse of barrenness. This attitude is readily understandable when it is realized that, as among the Anang, infant mortality exceeds 40 per cent—

miscarriages, stillbirths and deaths during infancy are usually attributed to attacks by malevolent forces. They believe that the power possessed by the Christian deity will afford them protection, allowing them to perform successfully this most important part of their role. (Messenger, p. 291.)

Catering as they do for urban needs, voluntary associations have also taken over traditional functions of social control. This includes supervising the private affairs of their own members. In Keta, for example, the pastor of a church is expected to settle the domestic problems of adherents, including matters relating to family dislocations or breaches of marital fidelity. An effort is made to reconcile the parties by arbitration in the lineage. However, if a satisfactory solution is not found, the pastor will certainly be the next resort. In more serious differences between non-kin members of the church, say, a member seducing another member's wife, it is considered un-Christian and therefore reprehensible for the aggrieved party to seek legal redress without first obtaining the advice of his pastor in the matter. (Fiawoo, 1959a, p. 89.) Many other associations have the same attitude. Thus, a Nigerian club in Freetown not only decrees that no member shall take legal steps against any other member without first bringing the matter up to the hearing of the meeting, but claims the right to submit evidence in court if its own arbitration is ignored by the complainant. (Banton, p. 190.) According to a report from Makurdi this kind of regulation was so effective among Ibo unions that Ibo people entirely deserted the courts except when drawn there by members of different tribes, or in the rare event of disloyalty on the part of a member of their own union. (Offodile.)

That an association is able to arbitrate in this way—even when the matter is quite unconcerned with the life of that particular body—is due largely to factors which have already been stressed. Its members have been taught to regard themselves as belonging virtually to the same family, and this feeling is carried as far as sexual relations. A Freetown *compin*, for example, sternly decrees that 'no member shall fall in love with any female member of the society'. Other associations have their own rules about marriage that their members are expected to observe, and societies with members of both sexes which arrange entertainment take particular care to prevent unchaperoned women being seduced. Measures to prevent trouble of this kind are provided for and one such group rules that 'any male member found guilty of adultery is liable to a fine of £1. 10s. 0d.; failing to pay this amount both man and woman will be expelled from the society entirely'. (Banton, p. 190.)

Such precautions may be deemed necessary because otherwise husbands would not allow their wives to attend and some fathers would forbid their daughters. Unless an association has a good reputation, it may be unable to obtain sufficient female members to carry on its activities. These and other disciplinary rules form part of the constitution which a prospective member must agree to abide by before he is admitted. This constitution which is usually written or typed in a book is extensive enough, sometimes, to take up nearly two pages of small print. In addition to the motto of the society, appropriate greetings and responses, there are generally the formal aims, lists of officers and their duties, regulations about membership, election of officers, etc. As the example in Chapter 2 (pages 39–41) has shown, there may be more than two dozen separate by-laws.

Allowing for local differences in custom the rules of most 'traditional' associations follow a common pattern. They prescribe a specific code of personal and moral conduct which is designed to regulate the public behaviour of members as well as their relations with each other. For example, a member who is reported for quarrelling in the town, for abusing elderly people, or for putting curses on others, may be suspended, fined or expelled. Similarly, in addition to adultery, where members are known to steal, or cause disorders at gatherings, they are warned to correct their behaviour. Very good care is taken that members are up to date with their dues and there are by-laws to regulate conduct in detail during the social as well as the business meetings of the association. Thus, in the dancing *compins*, a person may be fined if he or she refused to dance when called, or obstructs the officials. In other associations, members must not talk about their personal affairs or greet each other when business is in progress. They must regard what goes on in the society as strictly confidential. Members are also warned not to be unconventional or frivolous in the way they wear their dress.

Ordinarily, breaches of these regulations are dealt with by the committee. When there is doubt or difficulty over a case it will be referred to more senior members, such as the society's Patron or Founder, or the approval of a general meeting may be sought for disciplinary action. In the syncretist cults the situation is slightly different. There are priests who conduct the ritual, but other officials instruct the devotees in the laws and the general decorum of membership. One of them is virtually head of the cult, performing duties similar to those of a tribal chief or elder of a ward. As well as acting as the cult representative in lay matters affecting the welfare of the cult in the wider community, he also settles intra-cult disputes. Like the other associations these groups also hold their own courts.

In addition, of course, to these formal tribunals, there are well-tried and salutary methods of a traditional kind for checking anti-social or improper conduct. Banton has described how some of the *compins'* songs can wield the weapon of ridicule and ensure conformity with the association's standards.

> The shame of it, Ai Kamara, the shame of it!
> Ai Kamara bore a child:
> He had no sooner grown up than she made him her husband.
> Ah friends, let us come together
> And consider if this is what is done in Temne-land? [p. 175]

And Achebe's description of a tribal union, although fictional, is relevant for the same reason. Obi Okonkwo has returned to Nigeria after qualifying in the United Kingdom where his studies were paid for by his fellow members. Being financially in low water he needs time to repay the loan. The Union is proud of Obi's achievement and is disposed to be generous, until it learns that he is moving around with a girl of 'doubtful' ancestry. She belongs to a special caste with whom Obi's people at home are strictly forbidden to marry or mate. This is pointed out to Obi at the Union's meeting in such certain terms that he has no alternative but to withdraw his request. (Achebe, pp. 79–83.)

In fact, the association's practice of helping its own members with loans of money is probably one of the main sources of control. It enables the officials concerned to exert their authority more readily, particularly as recalcitrant members are sometimes the most needy. The ultimate sanction, however, lies in the fact that every reputable society is at pains to check applications for membership. They keep in touch with each other, partly for this purpose. Since they will rarely admit a person who has earned a bad name for himself in another organization, this form of ostracism may be very effective, especially if the individual concerned has little hope of companionship outside his own tribe.

Finally, by setting social standards in ways of this kind, voluntary associations affect the wider community. This is the case because in terms of their total membership they contain a not unappreciable proportion of the total urban population—perhaps as many as two out of every three adult inhabitants of the town in some cases.[1] They comprise literate and illiterate people alike, include men and women of all ages, sometimes children, and are not confined to any one class of individual. Very often their leaders are looked up to as 'progressive', and among their patrons and supporters are many persons who are influential and of high social standing. There are tribal chiefs and elders as well as professional men and women, clergy and educators and well known politicians. In general, their membership is representative of most sections of the wider community.[2] This means, therefore, that in substituting for the lineage and for other traditional institutions of kinship, voluntary associations perform a much wider function than the services rendered to their own members. They help to establish fresh social norms for society in general.

This is important because, particularly in respect of the urban family—the upbringing of children, marriage—there are few agreed patterns and moral standards are confused. According to which cultural values, for example, is an illiterate mother to prepare a daughter at school for marriage? Traditionally, a high degree of companionship is not regarded as essential and much greater emphasis is placed on the economic and procreative purposes of the institution. Western norms, on the other hand, stress a companionate relationship. Furthermore, after marriage has taken place, what is there to control

[1] For example, in Tefle, a small Ghanaian town of some 1,600 inhabitants, at a rough estimate about 68 per cent of the adult population belonged to associations (see Fiawoo, 1961, p. 107). See also the Conclusion (pp. 164–5, below).

[2] The social background of the officers of a Ghanaian youth association studied by Fiawoo (1961, pp. 11–15) exemplifies this point. He gives a table showing the education, religious affiliation, social status and sex of the office-bearers in question.

the behaviour of man and wife? Formerly it was the responsibility of the relatives to see that they observed their marital obligations. Nowadays, marriage having become an individualistic affair,[1] it is not rare that the kinsfolk of the one party are strangers to the kinsfolk of the other party. Formerly marital disputes were settled 'in the house'; both family groups had an interest in keeping the marriage intact. Now, it is no longer a union of two lineages or families and so there is no pressure on the couple to maintain the marriage. (Little, 1959b, p. 78.) Ideological as well as economic factors conduce to make the small domestic group based upon the conjugal relationship of man and wife, rather than the kin group, the primary social unit. (Baker and Bird; Little, 1959b.)

In contrast to this ambiguity, voluntary associations have a clear policy of their own. They may, as in the case of the separatist churches, compromise with traditional attitudes to the extent of condoning polygamy. But they all strongly support marriage as an institution. They do their best to remove causes of marital friction, and they strengthen the relationship of man and wife in various ways. Some of the syncretist cults, for instance, go so far as to forbid their members to divorce. If a member does wish to end his or her marriage, this can only be done with the cult's consent after a full enquiry into the whole affair. Most of the associations specifically condemn adultery and some of them discourage other forms of promiscuity by debarring 'indecent sex-play', 'co-habitation out of doors', etc. Abortion is treated as a crime 'tantamount to

[1] In the more extreme cases, the breakdown of traditional marriage leads not to a companionate relationship, but in the opposite direction. Thus, in Lunsar (Sierra Leone) where husbands have themselves supplied bride-wealth and have not carried out the customary obligation of farm service to their wife's father, they feel that they have 'bought' their wives. This is especially so with educated and literate men. As one said, 'The reason we despise our wives so much is we feel we have bought them' (Littlejohn).

murder', and special attention is given to matrimonial quarrels, including infidelity. Some of the women's groups not only upbraid members who create strife among other women but expel those who are constant trouble-makers in the home. Very often, these matters are dealt with by legislation, but there are the usual informal methods of social control. The following song of a Freetown *compin* was sung to a chief's wife when she was estranged from her husband:

'Oh Bom Posse, Oh Bom Posse, patience in marriage is a good thing,
Which God has given you,
When you grow old you will see how good is this thing,
Which God has given you'. [Banton, p. 174]

Other informal methods include a species of marriage guidance council. As mentioned below, church groups in this way try to get husbands and wives to talk their marital problems over together. They also give advice individually to their members. In addition, these church societies and many of the 'traditional' associations endeavour to influence the younger unmarried people, sometimes children, over family affairs. As mentioned above, one of the latter organizations—La Goumbé—appears to have taken the entire institution under its own wing. It restricts its female membership to nubile girls, supervises their marriages, and provides wedding presents and maternity benefits. More generally, as indicated in Chapter 7, associations also obviate problems of courtship.

To sum up, then, urban life is characterized *inter alia* by a specialization of function. Instead of being carried on by the kin group and the tribe, activities of the town are divided among a larger number of institutions. There are mines, factories, shops and offices to organize economic production and conduct business, schools to undertake education and the training of the young; churches and mosques have charge of religion; law and order are the responsibility of magistrates and of the police; and with the new emphasis on individualism the trend is towards the small elementary family. The voluntary association serves as an adaptive mechanism in relation to these new institutions by facilitating role segmentation. In other words, it helps to adjust the rural migrant to his fresh status as a townsman, as a member of a multi-tribal community, as a breadwinner and as a partner in a monogamous marriage. Further, since they help to establish and validate fresh norms and exercise control over the personal conduct of their own members, voluntary associations are one of the means whereby an over-all system of relationships is integrated and law and order maintained among the town's heterogeneous population.

The next two chapters consider the way in which the role-development referred to is manifested in the changed status of particular social groups.

6

THE RISE OF THE YOUNGER MEN

REFERENCE has already been made to the large part played
by the younger men, literate and illiterate, in founding and
supporting voluntary associations. These activities reflect
certain aspirations. As a group the young men are interested
not only in promoting modern changes and improvements but
in advancing their social position. Associations have assisted
this movement mainly in two ways. They have helped the
younger men to obtain a much greater say in public affairs,
particularly politics, and they have provided a general training
in leadership.

Both these changes involve a new status because in tribal
society the younger age groups are under the control of the
older men. Among the Mende, for example, the younger
members of the family are completely at the command of the
household head and are expected to work on his farm, collect
palm fruit, and press oil for him, re-thatch his house and keep
his compound in repair. They are dependent upon him for
subsistence and upon him and their senior relatives for bride-
wealth when the time comes for them to marry. A young
person is expected to treat elderly people, women as well as
men, with the greatest respect and deference and not to
approach them without genuflecting. Broadly speaking, his
social juniority obtains until a man is old enough to have
wives and to farm on his own. Prior to this, irrespective of
his physical age, he may be referred to as a small boy. In more
general terms, not only does the heavier work on the farm fall
to the younger age groups but they are also expected to perform
the more menial tasks about the village, and to answer the

call whenever one of the 'big' men has need of their labour. (Little, 1951.)

In the town, these family and other traditional controls have much less force, even among the indigenous population. Nevertheless, there are headmen and other authorities who wield a certain amount of jurisdiction over their fellow tribesmen. These people, who are usually elderly men and representative of the more conservative element, are the principal intermediaries between their own group and the civil authorities. The consequence is that although the younger migrant has relative freedom to come and go as he pleases, his everyday affairs continue to keep him under the eye of the older men, and may necessitate his retaining their goodwill. He may, for example, require a recommendation for a job; or he may need his tribal headman to stand as his surety if he breaks some local by-law, or gets into trouble with the members of another tribe.

Many of the younger men resent very strongly their continued dependence in this way upon their seniors. They regard it as particularly out of date when, to an increasing extent, they have been to school. Numbers of them have jobs which involve the use of modern machines and appliances; others again have visited foreign countries and seen people living in a more modern fashion. They are the more impatient because progress, as they view it, is being made by other tribes around them. They desire to follow in the tracks of other Africans, but their traditional leaders—the older men—are apathetic. There are none among them educated or enterprising enough to show the way.

Dissatisfaction is the greater because institutionally, in some cases, the role of the younger age groups was far from negligible. In southern Ghana, where prior to British rule there were the *asafo* companies, the young men had been warriors, the potential leaders among them no doubt officers and organizers. As individuals they were under the authority and control of the elders, but *as a group* their positions had been recognized. In doing away with the traditional organization, the British had deliberately destroyed the political function of these companies as well. Nothing appeared to take their place and there was a lack of opportunities of leadership in large numbers of men from 30–50 years of age. Although at the height of their power as individuals the age-group did not as a rule have any place of authority in the new power structure. (Ward, p. 58.)

In Freetown, a number of Temne migrants perceived that a way out of this kind of difficulty lay in reviving the prestige of their tribe. There being no solution within the indigenous framework of Temne society, some other solution had to be created which would also appeal to the younger men, whatever the attitude of the illiterate elders. A schoolmaster and a teacher of Arabic gave a lead to this new organization. A number of songs in Temne were composed and a new kind of swing devised. The schoolmaster was an advocate of European education and methods. Since he had already exposed corrupt practices among the tribal elders he was supported by many of the young men who were dissatisfied with such lethargy. The society that the schoolmaster and his associates formed was called the Ambas Geda. In Temne, *ambas* means 'we have' and *geda* is the Krio (Creole) form of the English 'together'. The name expressed the feeling that 'We, the Temne, have the people and we must bring them in', while its combination of Temne and English words unconsciously typified the blending of tribal elements with items taken from European culture. (Banton, p. 166.) Some of the Ambas Geda songs expressed the conflict between the older and younger generations as well as between it and a rival company:

Ah, look what is being said,
Look what is being done,
How they envy our play.
Ah, I do believe (in the play)
As the old folk envy the geda,
Let them just go on envying!

I've been done a bad turn, why?
Though not knowing me, they've
done me a bad turn, why?
The old folk have nothing but bad turns
up their sleeves. Hear me, Allah!   [*ibid.* p. 166]

About two years after the founding of Ambas Geda, one of its best and most popular members was expelled from the association for having seduced a woman on the society's premises. However, the officers gave him every assistance in founding a new society on similar lines. He gave it the name, 'Boys London', to make it appear the most civilized of all the companies, and soon it achieved something of the fame of its parent. Other groups were formed and the nine successful companies established branches, with the result that there were about thirty such companies in active existence in Freetown. In addition, there were at least another fifteen Temne friendly societies which were similar in most respects, though they had a smaller number of members and operated in a less ambitious fashion. (Banton, pp. 167–8.)

The significance of the companies is very evident in the recent history of the Temne. When, during the war, the post of Temne Tribal Headman fell vacant, the young men determined to put up their own candidate. Their choice finally fell on the schoolmaster who had taken the lead in forming Ambas Geda. He resigned office in the latter organization but intended to keep closely in touch with it and the other companies. The young men supported him because he stood for progressive administration and the elimination of corruption, and their final canvassing won many converts. Since campaign funds did not run to the hire of lorries, his supporters rode in the other candidates' lorries to the polling field. On reaching their destination they unfurled large banners bearing their own candidate's name, while 4,000 pin-flags were brought out of concealment and fastened in the clothing of their comrades. The members of the other companies outside Freetown were also brought in on chartered lorries. The latter were not entitled to vote, but such was the effect of the demonstration that the majority of persons present declared themselves for the young men's candidate. (Banton, pp. 176–7.)

The new Headman entered office with little support among the elders. Nevertheless, he was able to reinvigorate the Temne Tribal Administration and he has exercised an authority greater than any of his predecessors, despite his legal powers being less. Part of this influence he owes to the fact that the section chiefs in his administration take care to be on good terms with the companies in their territories (*ibid.*). The dancing companies have also been active in up-country towns. In several cases they have influenced the election of paramount chiefs by contributing money to the campaign funds of a young candidate who was one of their members.

In the above cases, the association concerned consisted mainly of illiterate and semi-literate people. The effect of groups of educated young men upon political development is more widely known. One of the first of these associations in Nigeria was the Young Men's Literary Association, organized by Nnamdi Azikiwe and others in 1923. About the same time, the Literary and Debating Society and the Study Circle appeared. The latter group sponsored essay writing, lectures, debates and book reviews. In 1940, eleven such groups organized the Federation of Nigerian Literary Societies for the purpose of improving literary standards and establishing 'unity among the literary societies of Nigeria'. (Coleman, 1958, p. 216.)

This type of associative development reflected the intellectual ferment of the times. A large number of these participants in literary activity emerged as the leaders of thought and opinion in the period. (*Ibid.*) Like their illiterate brothers many of the educated young men were impatient with their elders. For this reason, several of the more self-consciously political associations were formed for the purpose of emancipating members from the parties dominated by such older figures as Herbert Macaulay and Dr John Randle. The first of these was the Union of Young Nigerians. It existed only for five years but was succeeded by the Lagos Youth Movement, later to become the Nigerian Youth Movement. Under the leadership of Nnamdi Azikiwe and H. O. Davis, both in the early thirties, the latter association became the nucleus of the first Nigeria-wide nationalist organization in Nigerian history. After contesting and winning the Lagos Town Council elections, it turned successfully to challenge the fifteen-year domination of Macaulay and his National Democratic Party over Lagos politics and representation on the Legislative Council. (Coleman, 1958, pp. 224–6.)

This meant a radical change in traditional leadership; and as part of its efforts to achieve national unity, the Youth Movement organized branches in key centres throughout Nigeria. In some areas the provincial branches were local tribal unions which affiliated with the Nigerian Youth Movement, and in others they were West African Student Union branches which changed their names. By the end of 1938 the movement claimed a national membership of more than 10,000, and nearly twenty provincial branches in all parts of Nigeria, though predominantly in the south. However, following a split in its leadership, the NYM went into decline and the initiative in the nationalist movement passed into the hands of the National Council of Nigeria and the Cameroons. The NCNC was inaugurated in August 1949 at a conference organized by the Nigerian Union of Students. This followed a youth rally held the previous year and also organized by the NUS. (*Ibid.* pp. 265–6.) Thanks largely to voluntary associations, political development elsewhere followed a similar pattern. In the Gold Coast, membership of the Gold Coast Conference in 1938, itself a predecessor of the nationalist movement, was made up of clubs, unions, and other literary and social clubs in the country.[1]

Thus, through their association with nationalism and by serving as the nucleus of political parties, voluntary societies have done more than restore the young men's former function. They have paved the way for younger people playing a different role—that of actively planning the course of public affairs. However, this direct challenge to the indigenous order is mainly in the new industrialized centres. In the smaller towns and in the rural villages, where the pace is naturally much slower, voluntary associations are more accommodative to traditional authority. The young men concerned wish for modern improvements as well as to increase their own prestige and freedom of action. They believe that they understand and can handle changing conditions. At the same time, they are aware of the power of the older people and do not desire to become involved in conflict. 'Family' unions among the Afikpo Ibo have dealt with this problem by co-operating with the indigenous age-set system. Instead of antagonizing the elders they have worked with the senior sets. This is done by including the elders in activities which interest them, such as the raising of loans,

[1] Cf. Busia, 1951, p. 132.

while continuing to 'propagandize', largely along traditional lines, for other projects towards which the older men are less favourably inclined, such as the building of schools in certain villages. In this way the protagonists of modern progress hope over a period of time to persuade the elders to ensure projects which they propose at present. (S. Ottenberg, pp. 1–14.) But not all the Ibo young men have been so conciliatory. The Lagos branch of a union in Owerri province decided that too much money was being asked locally for bride-wealth. It passed a resolution to this effect and declared a boycott. Its members would not marry a girl of their town until the matter was remedied. This decision obliged the elders substantially to reduce the amount. (Comhaire-Sylvain, 1950b, pp. 235–6.)

Seeking thus to 'help and push' their people, family and town unions have been in the forefront of community development at every level. In other rural villages, in addition to promoting such modern enterprises as schools and construction projects, they have successfully pressed the local authorities for better roads, dispensaries, and other public amenities. They have also urged the democratizing of traditional government, and in some of the multi-tribal areas have been represented on Township Advisory Boards or Native Administration Councils. (Coleman, 1952, p. 215; Caprasse.) Likewise in Ghana, study circles and youth associations consisting of men and women of varying degrees of literacy have worked in the same direction. They have sometimes criticized the matrilineal system for being out of date (Ward, p. 49) and have tackled other modern problems in a practical way. Fairly typical of the latter kind of organization is an association which has provided its own small town with a new post office, modernized the police station, and cleared ground for further building. It has also taken over the complete administration of a day secondary school, including responsibility for teachers' salaries and school equipment. (Fiawoo, 1961, p. 116.)

It goes without saying that many of the 'Christian' associations also have youthful leaders, and young men have been active in forming new cults of the syncretist type previously described. Although not lineage heads, they may be called in for consultation in important local matters, such as the planning of a new school and the levying of local taxes to pay for it. (Ward, p. 58.) Similarly, it is the educated young secretary of a craft union or guild, not its traditional head, to whom members go for advice about their business. This new procedure derives from the way in which such groups have adapted themselves to urban conditions. For example, the goldsmiths of Keta who were originally a loosely organized group of craftsmen turned themselves into a local branch of a nation-wide union whose headquarters are at Accra. The Chief Goldsmith was not himself elected President because, being only semi-literate and unable to speak English, he could not adequately deal with headquarters. But he enjoyed much prestige among his associates, and they were unwilling to replace him. The difficulty was solved by electing the Chief Goldsmith Life Chairman, while an educated man was chosen as President. The Chairman refers to himself as the 'owner' of the Union, in much the same way as a fetish-owner draws a distinction between himself and the fetish priest; when he dies his office will probably pass down to his eldest brother, or to one of his own sons. The President, on the other hand, is freely elected by all goldsmiths on the basis of organizing ability and education, and his office is not confined to any particular family. (Carey.)

The latter case exemplifies the importance of new qualities and qualifications, particularly education. Otherwise, the fact that the younger men are entrusted with positions of responsibility merely recapitulates to some extent the traditional system. Attention has already been drawn in that regard to the function of age-sets and young men's companies. The difference is that not only young men as a class but young men as individuals now have a much wider scope and can make themselves publicly heard. Also, their influence is now exercised on a national scale. These facts are shown very clearly by the age compositions of the Nigerian political élite in terms of membership of the Regional Houses of Assembly and the central House of Representatives during the period 1951–7. The median age of the members concerned varied between the high thirties and low forties. There were very few over sixty. Among the regions, the Eastern Region had elected the most youthful legislature, with the median age between thirty-five and thirty-nine. (Coleman, 1958, p. 378.)

Voluntary associations assist this re-structuring of age roles in several specific ways. Firstly, although office within a given tribal union, society or *egbe* gives no formal status in the town, the qualities of leadership displayed by office-holders do not pass unnoticed. They earn a person prestige and esteem and may often mark out a likely candidate for a chieftaincy title or election to a local government council. (Lloyd, 1959, p. 52.) For example, there is the case of the Freetown *compins* cited above. The leader in question is now a Minister in the Sierra Leone Government.

Secondly, an individual holding office in an association gains, through handling its business, the kind of experience that is highly relevant to personal success in public affairs. This is because the formation and management of such groups demands not only youthful enthusiasm and energy, but the skill of an intermediary between the modern and the traditional world. The fact, for example, that the traditionally based associations consist very largely of uneducated people means that innovations have to be introduced with special care and due regard paid to conservative attitudes and prejudices. The leader may set, and is expected to set, new standards; but if he moves too fast, his flock will turn against him or lose interest. He must know his way about in the modern world, but it is equally important for him to understand the customary habits and outlook of his own and other tribes. Nor is it enough merely to pay lip service: he must show his respect for such things in his personal life—in daily dealings with his followers and in his treatment of senior men and of traditional leaders.

Since the latter factors place such a high premium on a tribal background it is generally in the first generation of European education that the mainspring of the associational movement is found. Such persons—mission school teachers, junior clerks in a government office, sometimes lorry-drivers—have two advantages. Although regarded as highly sophisticated they are still sufficiently in touch through kinship and marriage to be thought of as fellow tribesmen by the illiterate people around them. Secondly, it is believed that through their occupations they are in a position to exercise patronage in respect of employment. If, in addition to these qualities, the individuals concerned are sufficiently enterprising, good talkers, and 'progressive' in their ideas, they will also attract the other educated young men. In the final analysis, however, what makes mainly for success is the leader's ability to interpret what he has learned through reading books and newspapers, through work and through travel, in terms that are meaningful to the illiterate rank and file. A few short case-studies will suffice to exemplify these and other relevant points.

In the Ibo 'family' association referred to, the man selected as the president belonged to the youngest village-group age-grade. He, in general, approved of the traditional point of view of the village-group grades, and his selection helped to make possible good working contacts of the organization with them. (S. Ottenberg, p. 16.) Another tribal association leader—this time in Elizabethville—held office largely because he was well known and respected in the town. He was originally an immigrant but had resided long enough to be accepted as an established citizen. He was aged nearly forty, had enough education to become a medical auxiliary and was married to the daughter of one of his tribe's 'big men'. Another leading member of the same association was much older. Although illiterate and of little importance socially, he was highly respected for his wisdom. A mine of information on tribal history, he was consulted by everyone in difficulty over customary law, or requiring advice about his everyday problems in the town. A third man was influential largely because, in addition to having a secondary school education, he had built up a prosperous business. (Caprasse, pp. 62–8.)

It also follows from what has already been said that successfully to organize and lead an association may develop qualities that can be very helpful to an individual's career in other ways. The multiplicity of offices, and the extent to which the more popular movements are ramified in local and central branches, indicate the amount of administrative skill, tact, and knowledge of human nature that may be acquired. There is also the experience of recruiting a personal following, choosing trustworthy lieutenants and keeping their loyalty—all this may be valuable training, particularly for politics. Moreover, associations in general, not only the larger and more complicated organizations, provide these lessons. In the relatively simple contribution club, for example, the headman of a particular section bears the onus if anything goes wrong. He has the task of collecting the shares from his own members and is at the same time responsible for paying for those of defaulters and of reclaiming from them afterwards. When the shares have all been collected he nominates the member who is to receive the money and obtains from him a thumb-printed receipt. This sounds a straightforward and not too difficult procedure, but Ardener has shown how much detail the headman has to master.

In this club the total collection of one shilling shares gives a take-out of £12. 8s. 0d. This represents 248 shares, though not that number of members since many members pay more than one share. Once in every four weeks all shares are doubled and two members receive take-outs, thus for every share a member pays 5s. in every 32 days, or 4 Ibo weeks. Further five members receive take-outs every 32 days, therefore the cycle should continue for over 49 Ibo months, or approximately 4 years and 8 calendar months. Persons who pay more than one share can naturally receive one take-out at a time and thus they receive their additional take-outs on other weeks . . . [Ardener, 1953, p. 13]

In addition to practical experience of management—collecting dues, raising funds and handling committees—the holding of office in an association has a further advantage. It provides a person who is ambitious with the opportunity of widening his personal contacts. If, for example, he has the position of chairman or secretary in a well known organization he can get to know influential people by using the society's name. That this method of advancing one's career has a place in modern African society as well as in Europe seems to be demonstrated by the following story in the monthly magazine, *West African Review*. Its hero, Lyonga, is a government junior clerk who, like many other educated young men, knows that one of the quickest ways to better his position is by obtaining a university degree.

But it was not so much his work as a searcher as his social activities which brought Lyonga to the limelight. He had been a regular attendant at meetings of the Secretariat Club and had shown an extraordinary enthusiasm in its activities. It surprised no one, then, when he was unanimously elected as the Secretary, barely a few years later. What's in a secretary, you say? There is much in being Secretary of the Secretariat Social Club, whose patron was no less a personage than the Chief Secretary himself. It gave him access to Government House cocktail parties where the social élite of the big city of Lagos met. When dances were staged by the Club at the huge Glover Memorial Hall surely everyone would want to 'meet the Hon. Secretary'.

Press reports from time to time would feature his name as someone who had been present at this or that party the previous evening. Once, when he arranged a Club debate, had he not the honour of introducing the highest official in the land to the chair amidst the deafening applause of an admiring audience? Few people arose to popularity so rapidly.[1]

The story goes on to relate how Lygona rose from being a searcher of files to be directly attached to a senior official in the scholarship branch of the Secretariat. In this way he learned all about universities overseas and their conditions of entry; he was also able to make himself personally known to the Scholarship Committee.

Another tactic open to those who are anxious for more authority or prestige is to enlarge the association by attracting or incorporating additional members and seeking to start new branches. Thus, the leaders of the Afikpo Ibo association mentioned above reached an agreement with the village-group elders to make all young men of certain age sets in each village join their village unions or create such unions, and for these unions to become local branches of the parent organization. (S. Ottenberg, p. 17.) This kind of expansion makes the leaders themselves more widely known as well as locally more influential. It means that in such ways associations can be a major stepping-stone to a more important institution and this is shown by their functions in political development.

[1] 'The Secretariat Clerk', *West African Review*, Vol. 26 (1955), pp. 566–7.

Thus, when the Ibo and other Nigerian unions formed the basis of subsequently formed political parties, the young leaders of the associations concerned slipped naturally from those posts into the regional legislatures. Some of them, moreover, were elected as representatives not of an officially recognized party but by virtue of their position in a tribal union or similar group. (Cowan, pp. 32–3.) In fact, not only is mobility assisted in this way, but official position and leadership of a voluntary association often go hand in hand. It is quite common to find the same individual representing his chiefdom in a local government council, taking a prominent part in church affairs, heading the local branch of a political party, and organizing other groups—all at one and the same time.[1] (Little, 1955b, p. 223.)

Thus, the various functions which voluntary associations perform as political pressure groups and in acting as agents of social change not only reflect the new position of the younger men in the community—they are also an important means whereby the role of younger people has been developed to include achieved as well as ascribed forms of status.

[1] Fiawoo provides similar evidence. In one such case, the individual concerned—the grandson of a local paramount chief—was active in founding a youth organization and other associational groups in his native town. In due course, he was elected to represent the interests of the chiefdom in the district council and was appointed a few years later as the first secretary-general of the association he had helped to establish (1961, pp. 116–18).

7

THE POSITION OF WOMEN

AS in the case of the younger men, the organization of voluntary associations has helped directly and indirectly to bring women more to the fore in community affairs and to give them a political voice. Thus, in some cases, groups of women traders have exerted pressure on the authorities of the land; and since most petty trading and much of the large-scale trading, too, are in the hands of women the politicians found that their demands could not be ignored. (Comhaire-Sylvain, 1951, p. 183.)[1] Also, in addition to successfully urging improved amenities at local markets, women's groups acting on their own frequently achieved the provision of social services, such as schools, maternity homes, ambulance services, and the employment of a larger number of female nurses. Both in the western and eastern regions of Nigeria they showed themselves capable of opposing Government plans and policies which they found inimical. A women's union, for example, was chiefly responsible for the agitation that led to the abdication of the Alake of Abeokuta in 1948. Also, a growing number of women have become prominent in the political parties, occasionally as election candidates, but more often as organizers of associations and inspirers of and spokesmen for the social attitudes of women.[2] Usually, such pressure is applied in-

[1] See next note.
[2] Among the more prominent of these spokesmen are Mrs Funmilayo Ransome-Kuti in Western Nigeria, Mrs Mabel Dove in Ghana and Madam Ella Koblo Gulama in Sierra Leone. In addition to being a paramount chief in her own right, Madam Gulama sits in the Sierra Leone House of Assembly as an elected representative and is a Minister Without Portfolio. She is the first woman to occupy a ministerial post in a West African government.

directly or behind the scenes, because, apart from the political parties which have women's sections,[1] the groups which women form on their own rarely have political aims. Nevertheless, the fact that women are very numerous in the societies formed by men, as well as having their own associations, means that their aspirations do not go unheard. (Baker; Carey; Hodgkin, 1956, p. 91.)

In these and in other related aspects, therefore, the women have been breaking much the same kind of fresh ground as the associations led by the 'progressive' young men. It is, in fact, significant that in many of the new associations which have introduced innovations the main body of support has been provided equally by women and by men in the younger age groups. Anang Ibibio women, for example, believed that being Christian afforded them more opportunity for religious expression, for in the indigenous religion manipulation of the supernatural rests largely in the hands of men. Women possess no shrines and are seldom allowed to take part in rituals, although they may pray and sacrifice at the female fertility and farm *idem*. In the mission churches men and women worship together and are equally capable of receiving God's grace. The syncretist groups go even further; they favour women evangelists over men. This was the attitude of women of all age groups. The men—those who were young adults and middle-aged when missionary activity commenced—were

[1] About these groups Hodgkin (1961) writes, 'It would ... be a profound mistake to conceive of the women's sections of mass parties as pre-occupied with organizing picnics and *tam-tams*, admirably though they carry out these duties. In many areas women constitute an important economic interest, illustrated by the Ghana market woman who, when asked why she was going to vote replied ... "I am going to vote fish"—as a Lancashire woman might "vote cotton". They have also played an extremely active part in political campaigns, especially during periods when their parties have been involved in direct or "positive" action, involving strikes, boycotts, or disturbances, against the colonial regime, as in Ghana and the Ivory Coast in 1950' (p. 121).

receptive to Christianity mainly for a number of practical reasons. Many of them are interested only in obtaining schools, hospitals, and other material benefits from the missions. (Messenger, p. 296.) This evidence and other data, too, suggest that large numbers of the women and the middle-aged and younger groups of men have broadly the same kind of objective. They may start from different positions but they are equally anxious to promote social change. Both parties aspire to a better place in the sun.

This interest in re-defining their status arises because urbanization has rendered the position of certain classes of women less secure than under the traditional system. The reasons are paradoxical and Western Nigeria provides an example. There, recent legislation in terms of statutory (Ordinance) marriage allows a woman a new independence of her husband's lineage. It makes bigamy a crime and gives a wife the right to sue her husband on the grounds *inter alia* of adultery; the right to inherit property from him, etc. The drawback is that whatever the European Ordinance law may claim, the men, and society generally, still tend to regard a man's relationship with other women as acceptable polygamy. What often happens, therefore, is that some educated men are first married to illiterate girls under native customary law. Later, when they are able to marry literate girls under the Marriage Ordinance, they divorce their illiterate wives but continue, in some cases, the relationship. Quite frequently, too, a man under the Ordinance already has another wife or wives married under customary law; although this makes him guilty of the crime of bigamy in the eyes of the law he is not regarded as culpable by popular opinion. Nor, quite often, is there any public objection to a husband having an irregular union with a single woman. Popular parlance calls these women 'outside' wives, not mistresses or concubines. The children born to them are always recognized as their father's children by all concerned—the father, his kinsfolk, and society generally; and he often spends almost as much money on these women and their children as he does on his legal wife and their children. (Bird and Baker, pp. 115–16; Busia, 1950, pp. 42–3.)

The Ordinance wife may not be happy about this situation, but she rarely goes to court. Either she is unaware of the recourse she can in fact have, or else she realizes that public opinion is not yet sufficiently on her side for it to be worth while her pursuing the matter. In the élite groups of leading politicians, well known professional men, and churchmen, and for the completely traditional section of society, marriages must be legal and correctly performed under one or other system of law. But many urban marriages fit into neither system, and this means that a woman may also be deprived of her husband's property because, at his death, his kinsmen may claim the entire estate. This is quite apart from the claims that they are customarily entitled to make during his lifetime. Nor, since her marriage was probably made without family consent, is it likely that she will receive much sympathy from her own lineage. If she is left homeless and penniless, they will probably receive her and her children back, but only if she submits herself completely to their control; perhaps the very thing she is most keen to avoid. (Bird and Baker, pp. 115-16.)

In fact, few men are willing to commit themselves to a statutory marriage unless the girl has a relatively high degree of education and some social status. A less educated or illiterate woman may find herself a partner in the kind of irregular union already described. Many such 'outside' wives, married by co-residence and cohabitation only, are coming to be accepted. If, however, such a woman is living on her own she will lack that degree of security and status of the woman living as a member of the indigenous polygamous compound. Being isolated in her attempt to exist away from its support, she will be even more dependent upon her own resources, including the major part of the upkeep of herself and her children. Having regard, then, to the similar position of many of the wives themselves it is as though the minimal conjugal unit of the polygamous family were scattered, placing the mother concerned in the virtual position of the head of the household and her children's main provider. (*Ibid.*) In Koforidua, for example, McCall found that 78 women he interviewed in the market were supporting or helping to support on the average 2·9 children. Four husbands gave nothing to the support of their children by the women in this sample, and none of the women who were unmarried received any support for the infants from the fathers of their children. Two deserted women had between them 12 dependent children and neither of them received anything from anyone.

25 women received less than 2s. per day;
26 women received from 2s. to 4s. per day;
13 women received 5s. or more per day;
 1 woman received 2s. per month;
 6 women wouldn't say how much they received, if anything.
[McCall, p. 295]

Slightly more than half of McCall's sample were local women. Their situation emphasizes the general ambiguity of many women's position. By entering into a modern type of marriage or by migrating, they have exchanged family and other traditional forms of security for the prospect of personal liberty. However, as a result of the deal, they are more dependent upon their own resources.

Not surprisingly, in these circumstances, such women often seek an economic solution. They evidently feel that the only way of guarding against an unsatisfactory marriage, of off-

setting insecurity, and of supporting their children, is by
becoming financially independent. This fact alone, the desire—
as they express it—to be 'free', probably accounts in part for
the great popularity of women's associations. Women join
for a variety of reasons, but largely because membership helps
their quest for power, their economic interests.[1] In particular,
it assists a woman to trade. This is of paramount importance
because for the majority of women selling is the only way of
earning regular money. A girl with some education can now
find work in telephone exchanges, hotels, department stores,
offices, schools, and hospitals, but less literate women have
few opportunities of paid employment. When, as in some
cases, traditional forms of subsistence are closed to those who
are migrants, petty trade—in terms of a stall at the market, a
tray of goods at a cross-roads, or along the side of a busy street
—is the natural as well as the inevitable alternative. It is also
from the women's point of view a sociable occupation.
McCall, writing of Koforidua, a town of between 25,000 and
30,000 inhabitants, has summed up the situation as follows:

Whatever the scale of their trading, whether the profits be enormous
or trifling, town women are under a compulsion to trade. There is
an expectation that women will support themselves even after
marriage and that they will contribute to the support of the children.
In the old days and even today in the rural areas, a woman can do
this by farming. In the towns, farming is not always possible for a
woman who may be a 'stranger' and therefore not entitled to local
land, or if she is a member of a local lineage or married into one, the
town may have been expanded until buildings have been erected on
the fields formerly used for farming, or the distance from the urban
dwelling to available farmland may be too great to make regular trips
feasible.

[1] Cf. Jellicoe, p. 42. 'The desire for power in order to lead one's own life as
one chooses, and—as a necessary means to this end—the desire for economic
gain, the writer believes to be stronger among illiterate women in the Protectorate than is often believed.'

Furthermore, it is quite apparent that women if they have a choice between farming and trading will chose the latter. [p. 291]

The same author estimates that not less than 70 per cent of the adult female population of Koforidua is engaged in selling. However, since Koforidua is one of the few daily markets in Ghana outside the cities it is unlikely that McCall's figure represents the general situation. Gamble, for instance, working in Lunsar, Sierra Leone, which is probably more typical of the smaller-sized industrial town, found a much smaller proportion of women in trade. On the other hand, it goes without saying that not only are more women employed in this way than in any other occupation,[1] but they greatly outnumber male petty traders. Possibly the recent census (1960) misleads the student here by classifying nearly all market women as 'petty traders'.[2] Nevertheless, its indication that out of a total of 323,900 persons engaged in petty trading, hawking and peddling in the whole of Ghana, 273,120 (84 per cent) were women is identical with the proportion found in the 1950 census of Lagos. In Accra (capital district) the percentage is given as 88.[3]

[1] In Lagos, for example, women in petty trade were approximately fifteen times more numerous than women working as dressmakers and seamstresses—the next most popular occupation. This is according to the 1950 census.

[2] Hill, Polly, 'Markets in Africa', *Journal of Modern African Studies*, Vol. I, No. 4, p. 452.

[3] In addition to the thousands of small traders who throng the markets of Kumasi, Accra, Lagos, and the other large centres of commerce there are women who have shops and stores of their own. In Ghana, for example, practically all the collecting-wholesalers are women or stranger-men (Hill, *op. cit.*). Although not nearly so numerous as male retailers and buyers of produce, some of these women merchants carry on their business on an extensive scale. In the Eastern Region of Nigeria, for instance, they trade chiefly in textiles bought wholesale from European firms, a thousand pounds worth at a time, and sell retail, through their own employees in bush markets as well as in town. Others trade in fish or palm oil, own lorries, build themselves semi-European houses, and send their sons to Britain or the United States for their education. Like their sisters in petty trade, most of these 'big' women are illiterate or semi-literate. (Leith-Ross, p. 486.) It is also worth recalling in this

The fact that women are thus able virtually to monopolize the humbler branches of commerce is due partly to the custom whereby a husband may give his wife a small weekly stipend which she uses to trade and so support herself, or he may give her a sum of money at the time of their marriage and she is expected to support herself from that through trading for the rest of her life. A small amount will enable her to handle the inexpensive food products traditionally sold by women. With a larger sum she can buy and sell imported goods where the profit is greater. (McCall, pp. 290–1.) When, in the urban circumstances described, many wives are not given this start, voluntary associations are the main standby. They help to provide the necessary capital and to put the woman trader in touch with customers. (Marshall, p. 95.)

The mutual benefit societies concerned are able to assist in this way because their schemes are adapted to trading purposes. In Nanamei Akpee, for example, if a member urgently needs ready cash she may be allowed to jump the queue of weekly subscriptions and so receive her 'collection'—perhaps as much as £70—before she has completed her payments. This provides a very useful alternative to a private loan at a high rate of interest. Similarly, in a contribution club, a member can arrange with her headman to receive her take-out immediately, paying him a small proportion of the amount due to her. Should the headman be unable to fix a date for her take-out, she has the alternative of borrowing from the club's box fund, also at a relatively low rate of interest. Or, she may borrow the money from a private individual and sign an agreement handing over the rights to her take-out when it falls due. She must continue, of course, to pay her share in the club. (Ardener, 1953, pp. 135–6.)

connection that Peter Bauer (p. 31) mentions three Onitsha women who traded in partnership for 25 years and had an annual turn-over of £100,000.

Not only do these schemes make it possible for a trader to obtain cash at short notice or to accumulate quite considerable savings, but they are specifically organized, sometimes, for the purpose of buying consumer goods. In one such women's club the article in question was waist cloths. The share was 6*d.* a week, giving a take-out of £1. 16*s.* 3*d.* Should any member fail to use her take-out for the purpose of buying cloth, she was to be fined 2*s.* 6*d.* Needless to say, not all capital raising is on so modest a scale and some of the associations whose members deal in food stuffs are said to make loans up to £50. One such organization, consisting of yam sellers, helped women traders to purchase and transport yams from the farms where the produce was grown, some 100 miles north of Kumasi. Members of this association paid £5 for admission and the entrance fees of some 150 members provided it with capital for the season. Ten per cent interest, payable at the end of the season, was charged on every loan. (Bandoh.)

In addition to providing credit, there are women's associations which regulate trading practices in their members' interests. In Lagos market,[1] for example, there is a separate section for each commodity—fish, the different kinds of vegetables, cloth, etc.—and the women sit according to the commodity in which they deal. Each such section has its own *egbe* which discourages competition between women trading in that particular article. Such is the sense of solidarity—the women gossip together, eat, drink, and spend the entire day in each other's company—that it is said to be unthinkable for a trader to disobey her market *egbe* in this matter. Any woman under-cutting is ostracized by her fellows, who may even take a case against her, reporting it to the leader of the *egbe*, and if necessary to the head of the market. The *egbe* also sees to it

[1] M. J. Herskovits provides a similar example, though at a rather earlier date, from Dahomey (*Dahomey*, New York, 1938).

that no male trader deals in certain commodities customarily regarded as the business of women. (Baker; Comhaire-Sylvain 1950*b*, pp. 183–4.)

Sometimes, market *egbes* also attempt to buy in bulk for their members, thus obtaining produce from the farmers at a cheaper rate and saving the overheads of buyers. Somewhat similarly, a Bread Sellers' Union was formed in Sekondi–Takoradi when supplies were very short, with the object of acquiring flour and sugar from the importing firms for distribution amongst the members, all of whom were licensed bakers. Other Sekondi traders, mostly women, tried to restrict the buying and selling of corn, rice, yams and other vegetables to the members of their own Foodstuffs Sellers' union. Both these plans failed, although another association of women, the Fish Sellers' Union, was quite successful in its efforts to ensure supplies of the commodity in which its members trade. Some of the members of their union clubbed together in fours and sixes to raise money to buy fishing nets, which were sold to the fishermen on agreed terms. A fisherman who received a net sold his catch during the fishing season to the creditor group, and the value of the fish was reckoned against the net. If a fisherman was able to pay for the net in one season, it became his own, but he continued to sell his fish to his fishermen creditors who now became his regular customers. In this way, the women were able to obtain the fish on which their livelihood depended. (Busia, 1950, pp. 25–6.)

Finally, in some cases, women's associations have undertaken the production of goods for themselves. In Southern Nigeria, for instance, their societies have run a bakery, a laundry, a calabash factory, and a gari[1] mill. One of the most interesting of these, the Egba Women's Union in Abeokuta,

---

[1] 'Gari' is made from cassava.

claims a membership of 80,000 women paying subscriptions of 1s. a year. It operates as a weaving corporation, and it runs a maternity and a child welfare clinic. (Hodgkin, 1956, p. 90.) The latter association also conducts classes for illiterate women, and this service is provided by many other women's groups. It enables the people concerned to acquire a rudimentary knowledge of English or French. This is useful for trading because both the registration of goods and the necessity of dealing with wholesalers and customers speaking a different language are helped by literacy. Finally, of course, there are the numerous benefit schemes which provide the women as well as the men with a form of insurance.

Also relevant to the question of female independence is the fact that voluntary associations facilitate various irregular relationships with men, including prostitution. Such relationships are numerous in the larger industrialized towns where there are many adult males who are unmarried or living apart from their wives. Especially do men outnumber women in certain migrant tribes and this is also the tendency among groups of educated Africans as well as Europeans and Asians.[1] This preponderance of unattached men in the urban population places an extra premium on women. It provides certain categories of women with a market for their sexual services, enabling them to earn money outside marriage, through concubinage or prostitution.

Many women have migrated specifically for the latter purpose. They come principally from other towns or from more distant parts of the Coast. For example, in Accra these

[1] In Accra, for example, in seven migrant tribes the number of female migrants per 1,000 persons was less than 300. The 1931 census showed a ratio of 3·28 males to one female among non-Africans. (Acquah, pp. 32, 43.) From figures provided by the 1960 census the ratio of males to females aged 15–44 was 1·32 in Accra (capital district).

'Tutu', as they are called,[1] are mostly Ewes and Calabaris. The section of the town in which they live constitutes a veritable red-light quarter. They take up a position on the door steps of their houses, allowing the client to make his choice. 'Karuas', another group consisting of Hausa, Fulani, Moshi and Zabrama, cater mostly for the northern migrants. Their practice is to rent a small house in the *zongo* where they lodge and feed passing strangers.[2] When a client leaves at the end of, say, a week he gives them £5 or £6 as payment. Kotokoli women are a special type of Karua who are sent by their husbands to practise prostitution. In addition to making money as quickly as possible, their aim is also to have one or two children by a client and to take the children back with them to Kotokoli country. (Rouch, p. 81; Acquah, pp. 72–4.)

The above groups of women rely mainly upon their sexual earnings for a livelihood. Prostitution is their profession. There are many others who have extra-marital relations with men, either by personal preference or because it provides an extra source of income which can be conveniently combined with their trading activities. The latter individuals—'husband-less women', as the Mende call unattached women—very often travel about the country and from town to town as business and other interests direct. In a sample of thirty-four young women of this type in Bo, Sierra Leone, only nine had resided in the same town for longer than a year. Contacts with the opposite sex were made personally, in the ordinary course of trading, or through the medium of 'rarray'

[1] According to Rouch and Bernus (p. 233) this name is derived from the expression 'two-two' (two shillings, two shillings) and is indicative of the fixed price charged by this category of prostitute. See also page 133.

[2] These small 'hotels' are also places where the young men meet to talk and play music. This is a fairly common practice in Hausaland itself, and women whose establishments are patronized by wealthy and aristocratic clients enjoy a high reputation as fashionable courtesans; cf. M. F. Smith.

boys.[1] The women were remunerated by drinks and clothes, as well as cash, and where a group of women share the same house, the arrangements approximate to those of an organized brothel. The exception is that personal choice is exercised over customers, the sign of acceptance being a head-tie thrown over to the person accepted.[2] (Little, 1951, pp. 167–68.)

The other category of woman has irregular relationships with men not necessarily because she enjoys promiscuity for its own sake, but because from her point of view there is no satisfactory alternative. She may have been divorced, deserted by her husband, or her husband may have died, leaving her with children to support. Rather than be tied down by traditional marriage, such women—and this applies particularly to girls who have been to school—very often prefer a

---

[1] The term in Sierra Leone for 'pilot-boy'—a youth employed by a prostitute to solicit and escort customers to her (cf. Busia, 1950, pp. 96–7). Such boys if necessary often belong to gangs who roam the streets and markets and steal from stalls and shops. In some cases these groups are organized in the same way as voluntary associations of the traditional kind. Since, however, their function falls outside the scope of the present narrative, it will suffice to quote Banton's description of the Alikali Societies of Freetown. After pointing out that the name 'Alikali' is loosely applied to a variety of boys' societies which were formed to organize dances, he says: 'These societies ran directly counter to parental authority and the boys were often instructed to steal from their own homes. After a time the police forced them to confine their activities to enclosed premises, and magistrates in the juvenile court punished offenders who had Alikali associations. Since then these societies have declined considerably, for public opinion became aroused against them. A Temne stonemason told me how he heard that his son was spending his time with such a society; he made inquiries and found that the boy had been playing truant from school for nearly a year. He gave him a beating and took him to the Police Station where a policeman warned the boy that if he continued in such bad company he would end up in the Approved School. Next, the father reported the matter to the Jama after prayers in the mosque. The men went in a body to the society's premises and discovered, to his great surprise, that one of the alfa's sons was also a member. They broke down the society's shelter and warned them against any other further meetings. There has been a powerful reaction against the Alikali society and it has become a general scapegoat. It was even suggested to the commissioners who investigated the rioting of February 1955 that it was the Alikali society which was responsible for the looting!' (pp. 186–7).

[2] See also Nadel; McCall, p. 298.

temporary partner whom, if necessary, they can change at will. The ideal patron is a man of the 'senior service' class with whom she resides or whom she visits regularly.[1] Since it is possible in this way to acquire property and houses of their own, such women are relatively secure.

Women of this type, sometimes accompanied by their regular 'friends' or patrons, quite often frequent the better class dance halls, night clubs, and hotel bars. Also to be found in the 'bright light' area of the town are girls who act as hostesses or as professional entertainers or who work in shops and offices during the day.[2] Many of them are looking out for men and, since they invariably dress in the latest fashion and may be witty and sophisticated in their conversation, they attract plenty of attention. Their problem is rather to find the highest bidder, because the things the girls are interested in— the finest clothes, costly jewellery and expensive entertainment —are beyond the reach of most clients. Also, they are fastidious about how they travel about in public—a 'long' car of American type is almost *de rigeur* and some of the more educated expect a Western show of manners. Other women, also sexually attractive, are more accessible. It therefore becomes necessary for the girls concerned to show that they have superior services to offer. Competition is keen for this share of the trade.

Voluntary associations assist these would-be courtesans by helping them to advertise and by discouraging unprofitable

[1] Quite often, the relationship is of a semi-permanent kind and the women are the sexual partners of the men for the whole period of their stay in the country. The women must, however, choose their partners very carefully and take good care not to arouse gossip by affairs with other men. Attitudes towards such women vary, but provided their behaviour in public is circumspect and the patron is of good standing their position is not socially unacceptable. If there are children they are likely to be brought up by the women's own family, and treated as ordinary members of the community (see also Acquah, pp. 72–3).

[2] Sometimes known as 'Jaguars' because of their style of dressing. They wear transparent nylon blouses, short skirts and European footwear.

competition. This is done in Brazzaville by providing at the society's own expense musical and other public forms of entertainment. One of the girls, specially chosen for the quality of her voice, as well as her good looks, leads the singing. A high standard of elegance is aimed at and older women of experience and taste choose the girls' dresses and instruct them in deportment. These societies—they are picaresquely styled by such names as Violette et Elégance, Dollar, La Rose (incorporating Stella)—also seek a good name for themselves by limiting membership to carefully selected girls. There is a committee to regulate the association and it insists on proper professional conduct, including the avoidance of casual prostitution. There is also a common fund out of which members in financial straits are helped and their funeral expenses paid should they die. In the latter event, the society behaves as if it were the family of the deceased; that is to say, every girl goes into mourning, giving up her jewellery and finer clothes for six months, and at the end there is a night-long celebration in some 'bar-dancing' establishment hired for the occasion. (Balandier, 1955b, pp. 145–8.) These practices encourage the girls to regard each other as sisters instead of rivals.

Since they are able to pick and choose[1] their lovers women of this type are known in the French-speaking countries as *femmes libres*.[2] It goes without saying that the generality of women who live solely by prostitution are not so discriminating. Nevertheless, methods of safeguarding their members' livelihood and of providing mutual benefit are characteristic

[1] Balandier comments: 'Il est révélateur des bouleversements survenus dans la situation de la femme à la faveur de cette sociéte nouvelle qu'est la centre urbain; elle choisit alors qu'elle etait choisie, elle cherche à obtenir le plus d'avantages possibles alors qu'elle etait source de profit et richesse capitalisée, affirmant ainsi un véritable renversement des rôles' (1955b, p. 148).

[2] See, in particular *New Society*, 21 November 1963, pp. 4 and 5, for an interesting note.

of prostitute's associations in general. In Abidjan, for example, there is a regular tariff and no Tutu is allowed to charge a customer less than the price fixed by the president of her society. (Rouch and Bernus, p. 237.) These measures are necessary because the women vary in age, and, irrespective of the class of customer catered for, expenses are heavy. There is usually the rent of a room; a plentiful supply of new dresses is required; and many such girls employ boys to solicit custom or to act as a go-between. Also, unlike the women with a regular patron, the ordinary prostitute has little social security. As a result of her trade, she may have cut herself off completely from her home town and be unwanted by her kinsmen.[1] Since, moreover, such women are often fair game for criminal gangs, as well as being frequently in trouble with the police, they rely upon their association to intervene on their behalf with the authorities as well as in disputes with other women.

In addition to providing women with more economic power, voluntary associations also lessen the extent to which they are socially dependent upon men. One of the ways is by helping the younger women to make their own choice of husband. For the educated girl, admittedly, courtship may not be a difficult problem because there are various social functions —dances, school parties and outings as well as home-visiting— in which she may be allowed to take part unchaperoned and to get acquainted with a young man. The illiterate girl has fewer such opportunities. It is likely that she was bred in traditional

[1] Many of the prostitutes in Sekondi–Takoradi had no ties with home and had changed their names (Busia, 1950, p. 108). Prostitutes in Accra on the other hand seemed to suffer little, if any, disapprobation in the town. If they visited their relatives in the rural areas, however, they might be expected to 'purify' themselves before they were accepted back fully into the village life. (Acquah, p. 75.) Also, according to M. J. Ruel, Banyang clan unions in the Cameroons are at pains to regulate very carefully the conduct of prostitutes who have returned home (pp. 10–11).

circumstances which forbid a woman to walk about with a man or to talk and joke in public unless her male companion is a close relative or kinsman. Certainly, one of the apparent characteristics of the industrialized town is its disregard of many customary restrictions, but traditionalism as well as the views of stricter Moslems and Christians have still to be reckoned with. Nor have parental controls entirely waned, and although many migrant women tread the same primrose path as Ekwensi's heroine, Jagua Nana, there are other women among the more settled and indigenous population who desire a 'respectable' marriage. More realistically, perhaps, than the school educated girl dreaming of a monogamous husband,[1] they look for a comfortable home and children. They want a husband who will treat them well and be considerate to their parents— the life he leads outside the home is a secondary matter.

The advantages to young women of this type is that in a dancing *compin*, or some other such recreational group, they can get to know young men personally in a way that might ordinarily be very difficult. Providing the association itself has a good name, a girl can go there and mix with the opposite sex in relative freedom and without jeopardizing her own reputation. It is true that in most such groups the women and the men are organized in separate sections, partly because this arrangement is traditional and permits the older women to keep a stricter eye on the younger girls. The numerous recreational activities, however—weekly gatherings, excursions to another town, and particularly the Western style type of

[1] Tanya Baker who has studied the attitudes of Nigerian school girls writes: 'Most schoolgirls claim a desire for monogamous Ordinance marriage. As a second preference they give a desire to be the first and senior wife of a man who may subsequently marry a second less educated girl, who may play the role of housewife and nanny while the first wife works. The schoolgirls all counted themselves too valuable to become subordinate wives or "outside" wives. These statuses they claimed to be reserved for uneducated or divorced women, and therefore below the status a young educated girl should achieve.'

dancing—bring the sexes closely together and enable courtships to start in an easier atmosphere. What also helps the women's status in a more general way is their part in the running of a mixed association. Both individually and as a group women members have duties to perform which are just as important for the welfare of the organization as those of the men. They arrange much of the entertainment, cook and prepare food, serve refreshments, and there are various officials to supervise these activities. One of these women—the leader—is responsible to the head of the association for the girls' conduct. She is expected to report to him any difficulties that the women have not been able to settle among themselves. The fact therefore, that the sexes work together in the common interest brings home the lesson that the men's own enterprises depend upon the willingness of women to co-operate.

The latter point, coupled with the existence of women's own associations, has some significance for the social standing of women in general. It means that despite the major institutions—politics, business, religion, etc.—being under male control, many women are sufficiently placed to influence matters affecting them as wives and mothers. This is demonstrated by the attention widely given to questions of marriage and of the family. As already described, many of the societies concerned have definite rulings about marriage and they legislate strongly in favour of a stable relationship between man and wife. The fact that in the mixed associations women frequently share administrative responsibilities with men is equally important for female morale because in rural society women are often priestesses, heads of clans and lineages, and sometimes tribal elders. Illiterate women frequently have a strong sense of status,[1] but unless she is highly educated there are few

---

[1] Cf. Jellicoe (pp. 41-2). 'There is a marked desire in groups . . . to clearly define the standing of members with each other, and an acute consciousness of

comparable opportunities of leadership for an urban woman. Women's *esprit de corps* is also promoted by the holding of public rallies. It is a common practice for the women to assemble under their union's banner and to parade through the streets, singing and dancing as they go. Also, their meetings and convivial gatherings recreate the kind of sociable atmosphere in which most migrants grew up at home, and the frequent presence of educated women is an additional stimulus. For the illiterate members it emphasizes the social significance of their movement.

The advantages of this social solidarity from the point of view of women has already been shown. It helps them to arbitrate in their own affairs and it puts them in a better position for bargaining with the opposite sex. Since in these regards the women operate their own social system it is also of significance that voluntary associations assist women to compete for social prestige—not with men but with other women. This is the case because the urban environment emphasizes the social value of certain 'civilized' modes of behaviour. It stresses the desirability of furnishing a home in Western style, of bringing up children in a modern way, of being neatly and tidily dressed, of possessing particular social skills, etc. These and other 'progressive' practices are propagated by women's associations and it gives their own members an advantage. It enables them to receive instruction in modern hygiene and mothercraft, to learn sewing, crochet-work, and other new handicrafts, and to be up-to-date in etiquette. (See also Chapter 8.) True, the associations parade their members in a uniform style of dress, thereby keeping personal rivalries within check. But they also assist a woman to make the best use of her money in buying

how they appear in the public eye . . . This is probably one factor behind the desire to have as many people on committees as possible, as it gives these members a defined place in an interlocking hierarchy.'

material and designing dresses, and it is in this sphere—in the public display of new clothes, jewellery and other accoutrements—that the women principally vie with each other and seek to gain esteem.

The result, therefore, of these considerations is that women's status continues to be, in part, complementary to that of the men. It tends to be defined according to the particular social situation—according, for instance, to whether a woman is highly educated or belongs to an élite family. The voluntary association plays its part by helping to adapt women's role to the new ideological and technological requirements. In other words, its influence is in the direction of persuading not only society in general but the women themselves that they are persons in their own right. More specifically—and this is related to the needs of the urban economy—it encourages and to some extent enables women to act and behave more individualistically than is customary under the traditional system.

In turn, this re-definition of women's role is an important factor in the general re-structuring of roles involved in the emergence of a class system. The latter process will be considered in the light of the integrative function of voluntary associations in the next chapter.

8

ETHNICITY AND SOCIAL CLASS

WE have been describing the wider scope now available to the younger men and women in general. For the former group there are increased opportunities of gaining public recognition of their merits and the women are in a better position to emancipate themselves from traditional control. These changes do not take place on their own. They derive from the fact that African adaptation to the modern situation involves the assimilation of different social values. This is the case because (instead of status and rank depending, as traditionally, upon family heredity, age, and sex) political independence and the expanding industrialized economy have opened up a host of new and important occupational roles. Whereas previously, responsible and well paid jobs for Africans were limited to a very small minority—the ruling families and the intelligentsia of the Coast —opportunities now abound in politics, commerce, government and the professions in general. Energy is needed, and, sometimes, personal influence, but provided an ambitious individual has at least a secondary education as well there is a good deal of room for him at the top. The result, since there are now many additional ways of acquiring wealth and position, is that the town's population tends to be divided by occupational factors. Generally, there are three or four socio-economic strata which broadly correspond with the monetary income, political position, and educational or technical qualifications of their members.

First, in these terms, come the men who hold ministerial rank in the government and the highest posts in the Civil Service. Sometimes referred to as the 'new élite',[1] because

---

[1] My use of the term *élite* has been explained in the Introduction.

they have inherited political power from the former colonial administration, the members of this group have generally had university or secondary school training. Also politically influential, in some cases, are the well-established land-owning lineages whose heads often possess hereditary titles as traditional rulers. These families continue to be important mainly because of their personal following among the indigenous inhabitants of the town and of the villages surrounding it. They set standards which are in accordance with the people's own conception of life and with their traditional values. For related reasons, the principal emirs and other leaders of the Moslem community—the khalifas of the great sects, the Imams and men with the title of Al Hadji—are also to be included in this category. In addition, there are the 'old' families of the Coast, who in the British territories possessed wealth and position long before Independence. Their earlier members served in the colonial legislature, were frequently prosperous enough to have their sons and daughters educated overseas, and were usually the first Africans to practise at the Bar. Principally in Senegal, some of the earlier French *évolués* had an analogous position.[1] These particular groups, including families of Sierra Leonean and 'Brazilian' extraction, have generally continued their close connection with Britain and France. The result is that their descendants are usually more 'Western' in outlook and more at home in the niceties of European bourgeois behaviour than other Africans. For this reason, the men and women concerned are also to be numbered among the élite. The social function that they perform will be explained later. (Busia, 1956, pp. 429–30; Little, 1955*a*, pp. 263–88; Mercier, 1956*a*, p. 522, and 1956*b*, pp. 441–52; Smythe, *passim*.)

[1] The earliest Africans to receive French citizenship were natives of 'four Communes'—Dakar, Gorée, Saint-Louis and Rufisque.

Other members of the well-to-do class closely associated with the élite are professional men, and sometimes women, university teachers, prosperous business men, less successful politicians, and the senior Civil Service in general. These are followed by the rank and file of teachers and nurses, clergy, owners of independent businesses, and holders of minor traditional titles. In turn, come the junior clerks, artisans tradesmen, and semi-skilled workers in general, while the broad mass of petty traders, manual workers, market women, messengers and other semi-literate and illiterate inhabitants of the town bring up the rear.

These occupational differences are reflected in differences in living standards. The well-to-do families have modern houses furnished in Western style and equipped with electricity and other up-to-date appliances. Most of them use one or more motor cars and sometimes employ a chauffeur. Other servants are kept to cook, mind the children, clean the house and wait at table. For meals it is customary to follow a standard diet of indigenous foods, but various Western dishes are added, and coffee or tea is frequently served. Guests are invariably offered alcoholic beverages, particularly beer and whisky. These people are also very well provided with clothes, generally possessing several complete outfits of Western dress in addition to a large wardrobe of 'African' costumes of the highest quality fabric and embroidery. Their élite pattern of life is emulated by educated and literate people in general to an extent which varies broadly with the occupational scale. In Lagos, for example, among a sample of householders in 1959 the median monthly incomes of traders and business men, clerks, self-employed skilled manual workers, employed skilled manual workers, and labourers were respectively £20, £18, £15, £14. 10s. 0d., and £7. Professionals and civil servants together constitute rather less than 10 per cent of the population and have an average annual income of £472. In Lagos, earnings probably compare favourably rather than otherwise with other large towns.[1] This means, average spending power being so low, that differences in housing and other amenities are extreme. It means that the great mass of urban people live in rented rooms or occupy even more makeshift accommodation, often consisting of mere shacks made out of wooden boards and corrugated iron. (Marris, p. 71; U.N.E.C.A. paper, pp. 42–3.)

There are, then, in terms of this wide range of material achievement the ingredients of a class system, particularly as the criteria of prestige adduced are closely inter-related. Thus, wealth needed for purposes of conspicuous consumption is gained partly through political position which depends, in turn, upon education. Education itself being of general importance, the more advanced the educational qualification —e.g., a university degree—the higher a person is rated. Furthermore, to have studied overseas makes him a 'been-to', eligible automatically for a 'senior service' post, and so completes the circle.[2]

[1] Particularly for women, quite a number of whom are to be found in the highly paid professional capacity: 1376 as against 7404 men (U.N.E.C.A. paper, pp. 37–8).

[2] A 'high life' ditty about a girl's fondest hopes expresses this whole paradigm very succinctly:

> 'What shall I do to get a man of that type?
> One who is a been-to,
> Car full and fridge full
> [i.e. possessing a car and a refrigerator]
> What shall I do to obtain a man like that?'
>
> (Busia, 1957.)

Note also Achebe:

'A university degree was the philosopher's stone. It transmuted a third-class clerk on one hundred and fifty a year into a Senior Civil Servant on five hundred and fifty, with a car and luxuriously furnished quarters at a nominal rent. And the disparity in salary and amenities did not tell even half the story. To occupy a "European post" was second only to actually being a European. It raised a man from the masses to the élite whose small talk at cocktail parties was: "How's the car behaving?"' (p. 92).

The drawback, however, to this formulation is that in the general heterogeneity of urban life few norms are common to the entire community. True, male and female members of the élite meet regularly at public functions and visit each other's homes for cocktails and dinner. To the extent that they share the same way of life and the same set of business, political, professional and other interests, this group constitutes a separate social class and even a community on its own. This also applies to other Africans who, although less highly placed have many of the same social attitudes and interests. Apart however from these relatively well-to-do and well educated sections, including Westerners,[1] there is no one focus for sentiment or unitary system of values. The tendency is for social relations to be conceived of primarily in terms of the ethnic group to which a person belongs rather than according to social or economic criteria. In other words, at different levels a person thinks of himself in the first place as an African, a European, or as a Lebanese; or again, as a Yoruba or a Hausa, and not as a member of a social class. This means that tribal affiliation becomes progressively important as literacy decreases. Take the position, for example, of a highly educated, well-to-do member of a given ethnic group who has a prosperous legal practice and has sons at the university. These things may win the admiration of his fellow tribesmen, but he will only gain their full respect if he also conforms with traditional ideas of the 'big' man. This means keeping open house and entertaining all and sundry. It means that although such a person may drive around in his car with other educated people and drink with them at his club, he will not omit his kinship obligations. However poor or illiterate

[1] E.g., expatriate civil servants and other 'foreigners' from Europe and America, including business men, representatives of government missions, university lecturers, etc. For the sake of convenience and brevity, these groups have been omitted from the present formulation.

his own or his wife's relatives, there must always be room for them in his house or his compound. His educated wife, too, must defer to the older people. On her visits to his natal compound she may be expected to wear her oldest wrapper and perform with alacrity the customary obeisance and chores. (Bird; Little, 1955a, pp. 10–11.)

The result, since these are quite different ways of gaining prestige, is that the valuation of what is socially regarded as worthwhile is diffuse and ill-defined. It is blurred, on the one hand, by traditional ideas of status and etiquette, and complicated, on the other, by educated people usually being accorded specific marks of precedence. They may, for example, be sheltered from the crowd by the police, given chairs and placed in the front at public functions, etc. Nor is their own attitude consistent. Some members of the élite deliberately eschew tribal contacts except to the extent that they are necessary for politics or business. Such a person does not join a 'traditional' association and he would probably not allow his wife to trade in the market or own a bar. But there are others—the headmaster of a school, for instance—who do not think it odd for their wives to earn money in this way. What this amounts to is that the urban process has to be viewed partly in terms of segmentation. It means that the pattern of stratification showing a series of socio-economic strata tends to be split by several vertical faults (to continue the geological analogy) which may follow particular ethnic and sometimes Moslem lines.[1] (Banton, p. 97.)

To some extent voluntary associations increase the latter tendency towards segmentation by providing the migrant with a substitute for his home environment. They continually remind him of his duties and obligations as a kinsman and they trade for support on these attachments. For these

[1] For a general discussion see Mercier, 1954.

and other similar reasons it could well be argued that voluntary associations not only keep the tribal spirit alive but add to its importance.[1]

This might indeed be the case were it not that in the town tribalism takes on a different meaning. For one thing, being outside his tribal chief's jurisdiction, the migrant no longer pays the same fealty. The other is that, as we have noted, voluntary associations themselves are a means whereby he may identify himself with another tribe. He may take this action for the sake of prestige or in order to find security within a relatively strong group. In either case, voluntary associations assist the re-definition of tribal affiliation, and official government sanction in the form of census categories give it permanence and status. (Wallerstein, 1960, p. 131.)

What is more significant, however, is that by assuming some of the extended family's function voluntary associations diminish the importance of kinship roles and open the way for ties that are less diffuse and particularistic. (*Ibid.* p. 135.) Such a development provides a precedent for the principle of association on a non-kinship basis. It also facilitates the growth of institutions better suited to the migrant's need for security and protection in an urban economy. In such circumstances, since fellow workmen are of more help than kinsmen, the question of origin becomes of secondary importance. The situation is similar in the case of trading because the only sure way of maintaining stable prices is to enter into a solemn compact with fellow traders equally averse to being under-cut.

There is, therefore, every reason to suppose that in the

[1] 'All through this note on the social organization of the migrants in the Gold Coast, we have found . . . that the transplanted communities, far from being "detribalized" are, on the contrary, "super-tribalized". The town and mechanised life do not weaken their tribal cohesion but strengthen it. They do not lessen their pride in race, they make it ten times stronger. It is not class which is being born among these workers in the Gold Coast, but a consciousness of race which is being reborn, if indeed it ever tended to disappear.' (Rouch, p. 60.)

economic field the influence of voluntary associations makes for intertribal co-operation. Such figures as are available for membership support this. Thus, in the Gold Coast (1954) trade unions, generally formed by the employees of a particular firm or municipal undertaking, had in some cases more than 1,000 members; occupational associations sometimes ran into several hundreds. The latter included herbalists as well as taxi-drivers, tailors and blacksmiths. There are also associations of butchers and of sellers of textiles, as well as vendors of fish and vegetables. A few of these organizations are seemingly for people from a particular tribe or town, but by far the greater number apparently open their doors, irrespective of religion or tribe. (Clarkson; Acquah, pp. 82–6.) It is also interesting, particularly since membersip consisted mainly of illiterate women, that of 67 mutual benefit societies in Accra, 61 were open to any one (Acquah, p. 87). Also, so far as can be judged, societies of this open kind were just as numerous as tribal benevolent and improvement societies in other parts of the Gold Coast.

Additional media through which voluntary associations obviously assist integration are Christianity and Islam. Here again the statistical position is unknown, but it is presumably related closely to the size of the Christian and Moslem populations. The integrative effect is probably the greater because some of the associations based on Christianity are interdenominational and the church associations and Moslem societies concerned do not always exclude from their activities people who are not yet members of the faith. What is even more significant is that the new syncretist cults apparently make no distinction whatever. These groups naturally insist on their particular faith being regarded as the true religion, but they recruit members and preach toleration regardless of tribe. In the majority of cases the initiate is merely required to renounce such practices as sorcery. They bring together Christians, Moslems and pagans alike and enrol their adherents irrespective of literacy. They teach that breach of their rules will be punished by the cult's own medicine, and so universalist attitudes are encouraged by supernatural sanctions: 'members are enjoined to pray for the well-being of mankind, including their enemies'; 'it is the duty of members to help others, alert those in imminent danger and extricate those in difficulties', etc. Moreover, such cults are essentially eclectic. Their treatment of magico-religious concepts, their ritual practices, their style of dancing, are sufficiently basic in structure to appeal to Africans of every type, not merely to a particular tribal element. Indeed, some of the more vigorous messianic cults expressly discredited such differences and actively sought to impress on their adherents that they were fellow Africans and not only cult members.

The latter point is a reminder that nationalism itself is another powerful force which has worked in the same integrative direction. This was the case because in their efforts to create a popular movement the more militant leaders accused the tribal chiefs of being adjuncts of the colonial system. They contended that the way to political freedom lay in Africans coming together in a single united body. This encouraged a revolutionary attitude towards the colonial regime. It was also an attack on the traditional norms and values which supported parochial sentiment. As such it convinced few people except the intellectuals and their immediate followers. Nevertheless, some seeds were sown, even outside the larger cities, and later, with Independence and the growth of parliamentary government, the building up of a completely new set of loyalties became a practical problem. A new sense of solidarity, based upon the party, had to be substituted for the solidarity based upon the older, more restrictive groupings associated with kinship, locality, language, and religion.

To this end, and to create a sense of the 'historic role' of Africans in general, an extensive programme of propaganda, mass meetings and rallies, ceremonials and rituals, the popularization of particular symbols—the RDA elephant, and the CPP red cock, as well as literature—have all been used. (Hodgkin, 1961, pp. 133–4.) The political parties have also sought to provide for the social needs of their members and supporters by assuming 'welfare' functions. In these and in other ways, the party branch offers the advantage of sociability and provides through its political discussions a new kind of combined group. And, over and above the minutes, reports and agenda, such meetings can be a very pleasant and friendly occasion. (*Ibid*. p. 83.) True, many voters are entirely apathetic except at the time of an election, and it can also be argued that since several major parties have a largely ethnic foundation— in Nigeria, the Action Group, the NCNC, and the NPC—the effect of political parties is merely to bring tribal particularism up to date. Nevertheless, the general effect is to widen the mental horizon. It means that millions of Africans have now through party membership a much broader affiliation which is sometimes emphasized by a solemn oath of allegiance.

The part played by voluntary associations in this regard has already been mentioned. Old Boys' societies and groupings, and even sports associations, have assisted the formation of mass parties, in some cases providing the organizational core. At its inauguration the NCNC, for example, was to a large extent a federation of tribal unions and improvement associations. Other types of organization, too, have had a formative influence, including the Matswanist Church in the Republic of Congo and a farmers' union, the Syndicat Agricole Africain, in the Ivory Coast. The latter provided the nucleus around which PDCI–RDA was organized. Trade union leaders helped Sékou Touré to transform the PDG–RDA into an effective mass party, and in Ghana the CPP grew up out of the Committee on Youth Organization. Literary societies, study circles, research groups, and other associations of intellectuals have been another source of stimulation. (*Ibid.* p. 47.) In these respects not only do the voluntary associations help to establish branches and supply speakers with a public forum, but they provide a network of communications through which ideas, information and directions can be diffused from the great towns to the bush. They organize demonstrations, the women members wearing party colours and dancing; and through the medium of *griots* and other traditional entertainers they spread propaganda. (Holas, 1953; Hodgkin, 1961, p. 87.)

Another widespread form of activity is outdoor recreation. Although on an obviously different plane from politics and religion, sporting associations also recruit their members irrespective of ethnic or tribal origin. They include, as already mentioned, clubs at which such games and sports activities as tennis, hockey, cricket, horse-racing, polo, and football (soccer) are played or organized. The best example, undoubtedly, is the last mentioned. Not only is football the principal form of leisure-time pursuit enjoyed by young men in general, but the typical club opens its doors to every kind of support. In an up-country Sierra Leone town, for instance, one such team, which had a Lebanese trainer, was drawn from a variety of occupations—office clerks, skilled and unskilled workers—and from half a dozen different tribes. (Gamble.) Quite often, membership is socially and ethnically mixed in this way because the clubs are formed by the employees of particular commercial houses, government departments, and banks. Not only are expert players much in demand, but the larger clubs have to rely largely upon public support. It would be more difficult, therefore, to raise the necessary finance for equipment, hire of a ground, and other expenses if they appeared to discriminate against particular sections of the community.

Football, then, tends to be an important integrating factor; the more so because 'team-spirit' is deliberately stimulated, off as well as on the field, by socials and by other familiar means. Some of the teams concerned adopt the names of famous English clubs. Others take such picturesque titles as Mighty Poisons, Great Titanics, Congo Vipers, etc. (Busia 1950, p. 158), with the object perhaps of overaweing their opponents as well as inspiring pride and confidence in their own players and supporters.

It is thus clear that, to a varying extent, trade associations, religious and cult associations, political parties, and sporting associations are all functional for unity.[1] By lessening the

[1] One of the earliest students of African urbanization to draw attention to similar factors was Ellen Hellmann, who wrote: 'Urban native life is subject to an enormous complexity of outside agencies and stimuli emanating from the social, economic, legal and religious institutions of a securely-established European culture. Passing reference has already been made to the influence of missionary bodies and of European economic and educational institutions. That the Communist Party programme makes a great, even if not permanent and unifying, appeal to the urban Native is not to be doubted. The influence of the Press, both European and Bantu, is inducing a more alert Native political consciousness. There are in existence numerous associations of Native herbalists continually engaged in raising funds to send delegations to interview Ministers and request the legalization of their status. Mission societies, by organizing women's clubs and circles, are introducing new forms of social integration. The Pathfinder and Wayfarer organizations provide forms of healthy co-operative recreation to divert the restless energy of undisciplined adolescents. Sports clubs provide new forms of organized recreation. The kaleidoscopic succession of concerts, meetings, and dances in location communal halls provides a valuable index of the direction, scope, and importance of communal activities. Some of these new forms of social, political, and economic enterprise, such as the Inchcape dance hall, the Gamma Sigma debating society, or the more recently established co-operative trading stores, are directly based on European models. Others, such as Pathfinder and Wayfarer organizations and women's mission clubs, are directly dependent for survival on European initiative and leadership. The stockfair, Native separatist churches, the social

importance of traditional roles they counteract the tendency towards segmentation and render social relationships more fluid. Associations consisting of educated members of society and the élite carry this process a step further. Not only do they recruit Africans of different nationality and tribe, in some cases they also cater within the same organization for Europeans of similar official and professional status. This social intermingling is important because, as Smythe has pointed out out in reference to Nigeria:

On the job in government or business the nature of work brings the men into contact; but this type of relationship is rarely carried outside the office; once the day is over, each goes his individual way back to his separate circle of friends and acquaintances. Since the character of the working day either allows no break at mid-day or, where it does, the pattern long established provides for a siesta at home, the opportunity even to have lunch together is obviated. Besides, Nigeria has almost no conveniently located restaurants or dining rooms serving a general public or specializing in non-African foods that Europeans prefer (there are a few expensive European-type hotels in larger cities). Thus there is little opportunity for Nigerians or Europeans to develop a friendly relationship from eating out together casually. At the same time, job resentment on the part of both raises a barrier; the Nigerian may feel that he is treated unfairly and held back, while the European resents the encroachment of Nigerians in what have traditionally been 'European' positions; neither is characteristically generous in his appraisal of the competence and dedication of the other. [Smythe, p. 126]

In addition to the professional association and groups which

functions arranged at communal halls, though perhaps inspired by a European pattern or responding to a new situation caused by contact with Western culture, are co-ordination of Bantu and Western practice' (pp. 432–3).

[Note also Gluckman's reference to Central Africa: 'Tribalism acts, though not as strongly, in British towns: for in these, Scots and Welsh and Irish, French, Jews, Lebanese, Africans, have their own associations, and their domestic life is ruled by their own national customs, but all may unite in political parties and in trade unions or employers' federations. Tribalism in the Central African towns is, in sharper form, the tribalism of all towns' (p. 65).]

meet for dining purposes a number of social clubs are even more international and cosmopolitan. The well-known Island Club in Lagos, for instance, is a resort for politicians, artists, journalists, and university teachers as well as professional and business men. Europeans, Lebanese and Americans mingle freely with Nigerians and other Africans, dancing, drinking and conversing. Provided a person is socially acceptable and can afford the dues there is no bar to membership. Nor are eyebrows raised if an African woman goes there escorted by a European or a European woman is in the company of Africans.

In thus encouraging fraternization, social clubs set a pattern of inter-racial and inter-tribal behaviour which bears the imprint of the élite. Its effect is likely to be the greater because, unlike the dining club, which meets in relative seclusion, the activities of these larger social centres are well-known and, to some extent, publicly visible. What is sociologically significant, however, is not that such behaviour symbolizes amicable relations between black and white, it is rather that in many people's eyes Europeans are the 'archetypal' strangers, psychologically and culturally more removed than the most alien type of African. To consort, therefore, with Europeans as equals, to treat them in the same way as Africans, takes particularism to its ultimate conclusion. It denies ethnicity completely and in so doing it paves the way for the associations' final function—that of crystallizing feelings of social class.

Voluntary associations take the first step in this direction by increasing interaction among people interested in Western ideas and ways. This is important sociologically for reasons of morale. Not only are the men and women concerned a relatively small minority, but their novel outlook and aspirations are regarded with skepticism by many Africans. The attitude towards them is not necessarily hostile, but it is frequently coloured by doubt and suspicion to the extent of separating them psychologically as well as socially from the ordinary tribal person. University students in Ghana have verbalized their reaction and their own feeling of being 'different' in the following terms:

'I find it takes my people a few days to get more close to me. They consider me as a man from a different world now.'

'Friends and relatives are obsessed with some inferiority complex which results either in fear or hatred.'

'Old friends find it difficult to talk informally to me; instead they say, "Mr. X, Y, Z", "Yes, Sir", etc. These expressions make me rather uncomfortable.'

'... the people around me have different views about everything, and our ideas and views always collide.' [Jahoda, II, p. 76]

Social clubs and recreational centres help to reduce this sense of isolation. Particularly in the small rural towns, they may be the principal means whereby an educated individual can keep in touch with the outside world and enjoy the company of like-minded people. The persons concerned become more conscious of sharing common values and a similar outlook on life. The effect, therefore, does not stop at moral reassurance. It may manifest itself in practical ways, such as providing educated persons with hospitality when they arrive in a strange town. (Little, 1955b, p. 225.) It thus involves the development of a distinct *esprit de corps* peculiar to such individuals as a section of society on their own.

This sense of solidarity is important psychologically. It is significant for social class because it makes for concensus, thereby enabling educated people in general to define criteria of prestige for themselves. Their aims are cast largely in terms of political power, social position, and professional status. Among the remainder of the population, however, the situation is not so concretely resolved. Many new opportunities potentially exist—political, religious and occupational. These constitute alternative activities in which an individual may participate, but common agreement about their social worth is lacking.[1] Not even wealth is a certain criterion because a man who makes money illegally, say, by illicit diamond-mining, is not necessarily condemned. Provided he spends the profit hospitably and in other socially approved ways, he may still gain public esteem. It may be just as great as that of men with an orthodox source of income.

What makes a difference to this indeterminate situation is that voluntary associations have clear rules of conduct and are able to enforce them. By insisting on the desirability of certain practices they set standards of social achievement and mark out their own members as persons whom it may be worthwhile emulating. The effect, in other words, is to institutionalize social differences and so to assist class formation.

The reason why 'Christian' and cultural societies are able to arbitrate in this way has already been explained—they aim at moral or intellectual uplift and point in the direction of 'progress'. The more popular organizations, such as ethnic unions, fit into a similar picture. They represent the older traditions, but claim to have brought them up to date. The members of élite associations are imitable largely because they personify in terms of university degrees and other educational qualifications the high prestige of Western technology. Also, having been associated historically with the colonial regime they symbolize, particularly for the masses, upper class ways and habits. Moslem groups and societies appeal for somewhat similar reasons. Not only did Islam also play a conquering role in days gone by, but Islamic institutions

[1] One of the complicating factors is that an individual evidently tends to over-rate his own occupation and occupations closely associated with it. *Vide* Gamble's unpublished study of the prestige of different occupations in the mining town of Lunsar, Sierra Leone.

now predominate in even larger regions of West Africa, including some sections of the industrialized towns.

The result is that voluntary associations and the embryonic social system mutually reinforce one another. The more an association is composed of the élite, the higher it is rated among literate people in general and the greater its impact upon people with similar Western tastes. Since quite a large number of such organizations directly or indirectly restrict their member- ship, this means that social distance is enhanced between educated persons themselves and not only between educated and non-educated. Thus, professionals are invariably affiliated with their general professional societies, such as Bar Associa- tions, Medical Societies, and Union of Teachers. A member of a university staff associates with the society of his speciality and, as already mentioned, there are unions consisting of the 'old boys' of the same school. Those in government Civil Service have in general two kinds of organization: a white collar union of Civil Service workers and departmental clubs within the various government secretariats. Men on the senior levels of government service rarely participate in either of these departmental organizations. As already explained, they and their wives have their own more exclusive groups in which, the aim being to recapture the social atmosphere of a high- class club in Europe, the meals taken together tend to be highly formal. Such is the prestige of these mixed dining clubs that the allocation of 'African' vacancies is said to engender fierce competition among socially ambitious women. Other élite organizations in which membership is restricted include the Reformed Ogboni Society; and persons wishing to belong to clubs concerned with horse-racing have to be rich enough to afford it.

Nor are conventional behaviour and exclusiveness confined to the educated class, because many of the traditionally based associations gain their reputation in a similar way. Thus, as reported above, the most highly regarded Sierra Leone *compins* are those with the strictest rules. Next come the other companies and after them the benefit societies, which resemble them in limited respects. Tribal dancing societies come lower down and informal dancing groups are at the bottom. In Freetown, at any rate, it appears that prestige attaches to associations the more they copy certain European practices, the more Islamized they are, and the more they call upon valued elements in the traditional culture of the tribe concerned. The Islamic element is important as representing the alternative to the magical basis of indigenous associations, for while the 'progressive' young men look down on the latter societies, they seem to be a little afraid of their 'medicine'. (Banton, pp. 191–2.) Indeed, in more general terms, the social standing of these and other 'traditional' associations—their ability to attract members—is frequently bound up with tribal affiliation. This is because certain ethnic groups and tribes—the Yoruba and the Hausa of Nigeria, the Mandinka of Senegal, for instance—are looked upon as more civilized or 'advanced' than others.[1]

Syncretist groups are in a very similar position. Missionary teaching places the indigenous religions at the bottom of the social scale, but these new cults incorporate Christian ritual

[1] Note Wallerstein (1960) in this connection. Sometimes, the definition of the ethnic group may even be said to derive from a common occupation—indeed, even does—rather than from a common language or traditional polity. For example, an Accra man often tends to designate all men (or at least all merchants) coming from Savannah areas as 'Hausamen' . . . such designations may originate in error, but many individuals from Savannah areas take advantage of this confusion to merge themselves into this grouping. They go, for example, to live in the Sabon Zongo (the Hausa residential area), and even often adopt Islam, to aid the assimilation. They do so because, scorned by the dominant ethnic group of the town, they find security within a relatively stronger group (Hausa in Accra, Dioula in Abidjan, Bambara in Thiès), with whom they feel some broad cultural affinity. Indeed, assimilation to this stronger group may represent considerable advance in the prestige-scale for the individual (pp. 132–3).

and theological precepts as well as traditional practices. They have a sound moral background, not unlike Christianity; there is an appeal to individual conscience and Sunday observance. Members are obliged to have no dealings with charms or non-therapeutic medicine, or have recourse to diviners. This creates the impression that their status is comparable to one of the Christian sects or denominations. It means that pagan members with no interest in church or Christianity feel socially elevated since they consort with Christians and believe they follow Christian ritual in all respects. Nor does it necessarily occur to church members that membership of a cult violates their Christian adherence. It is association with indigenous magico-religious practices which abases or reduces one's status and invites the sanctions of the church. (Fiawoo, 1959*b*.) Again, one of the main reasons for Christianity's own prestige is that it is popularly regarded as a major civilizing force. This automatically gives the church societies and associations a special rating. However, the individual position on the social scale depends very much on the extent to which a particular denomination or church *egbe* has the élite's support. (Lloyd, 1959, p. 53.)

Freetown society illustrates both these points because from the start Sierra Leone was conceived as a centre from which Christian and civilizing influences could be spread into the interior of Africa. With evangelization and commerce going hand in hand there grew up a relatively prosperous and highly Westernized class of Africans who felt themselves much superior to tribal migrants from the interior. The members of this Creole community (as it was subsequently called) also made distinctions among themselves. Those who derived from the original settlements looked down upon those who had been liberated from the slave ships. Since, however, Christianity continued as a paramount force, a family was able to better its social situation through church affiliation. It might move, as its material position improved, from a smaller to a larger church, from independent chapels to mission churches, and from Wesleyan chapel to the Anglican Cathedral. (Porter, 1953, pp. 11–13, and 1963.) Later, families from up-country acquired education but found that in order to obtain respected employment it was necessary to change their names and 'pass' as Creoles. Many Protectorate people seeking to advance their status placed their children in Creole families as wards, and membership of a Creole friendly society assisted assimilation.

More recently, Islam became a powerful force among the tribal population of Freetown, but in the formation of this Moslem group the indigenous Temne were at a disadvantage, for the more orthodox and wealthy tribes like the Aku, Fula and Mandinka, were accorded a higher prestige than the partly pagan and poorer tribes. The result was that Mandinka dancing *compins* became very popular because they provided a means whereby ambitious youths could identify themselves with a more 'civilized' group than their own. (Banton, pp. 103–4, 163–4.) By taking part in the society's activities, including Mandinka songs and dances, many of them learned the language and to comport themselves like Mandinkas.

The fact that voluntary associations help social adaptation in this way—by assisting people to acquire the habits and mannerisms associated with a higher status—has implications for upward mobility in a general sense. In particular, it benefits the newly educated class, because most of the young people seeking the good jobs now available in the Civil Service, the government and the professions were reared in tribal homes. Even among students at the new universities it seems to be rare for a person to have more than one parent who is literate and in an appreciable number of cases both parents are illiterate. (Jahoda, II, pp. 71–2.)

These young people have considerable ambition. But their expectations of arriving quite quickly at the top rung of the occupational ladder tend to be unrealistic. They do not initially realize that more than long hours of study and satisfactory examination results is needed to compensate for the disadvantages of a tribal background. Particularly if the person concerned is required simultaneously to adjust himself to two different worlds—family, friends and neighbours at home, as well as his career—the extent of his self-confidence and general sophistication may be insufficient for the position aspired to. A few years ago a college graduate enjoyed a seller's market for his abilities; now, as the number of graduates increase, the shortage of highly trained personnel begins to abate. With increasing competition there is likely to be a greater interest in personal, as opposed to formal, qualifications. (Smythe, p. 173.)

Women feel this lack of self-assurance even more keenly than the men, mainly because they are generally behind their husbands in education. Also, the modern situation demands more socially of a woman, especially the wife of a successful man. Today, instead of remaining in the background or retiring to the women's quarters, she is expected to play the hostess when his friends or business associates arrive. Failure to perform these new functions will put her at a disadvantage with more sophisticated women, African as well as European, since it may detract from the husband's own prestige. Largely for this reason a number of men are very careful to choose a girl who has been trained in Western ways. Ideally, she should have travelled widely and finished her education overseas, and girls brought up in the 'old' families of Freetown and Lagos have been much in demand. Such marriages are contracted entirely among the élite; but many less socially prominent men, also, would be embarrassed if their wives were unable to entertain their guests in Western style. Quite often, therefore, a tribal chief or an illiterate trader wealthy enough to support a polygamous household includes a literate woman as one of its members. Her role is to cook meals to the taste of his educated visitors, as well as to write his letters. (Phoebe Ottenberg, p. 213.)

That women are alive to this situation is shown by the relatively large amount of space given to social matters in the popular press. For example, several leading newspapers in Nigeria carry once a week a column that includes social notes. There are references to well-known personalities and 'socialites' and to persons going overseas. These articles discuss the proper kind of relationship between persons of different sex and there is frequently a column answering readers enquiries about etiquette. Among the problems raised are such apparently trivial questions as how much food a person who is a guest can leave untouched on her plate; when it is proper for the veil a bride wears over her face to be lifted, etc. Advice on how to play the host or hostess is frequently given, and one such article warned the housewife against meeting guests in her kitchen clothes. She was advised to have food prepared in readiness for them and to see that utensils and tumblers were clean; it pointed out that the husband as well as the wife has duties as a host. Fashion notes and dress-making hints are also provided as a regular feature, and photographs of African women illustrate the use of cosmetics. Not long ago a monthly magazine which is read by African students overseas as well as by educated people in the Coast offered detailed advice about deportment. After explaining how a woman can sit elegantly on a low seat when wearing a tight skirt, or sit cross-legged on a straight seat, this article warned against standing akimbo as it displays too much of the hips. It went on:

... the West African woman still has something to learn from the deportment schools of London and Paris. She can learn, like the girls in Europe, that a large stride has something of the masculine quality about it; a small one, feminine charm ...

What other things does a girl who wants to charm and please and be acceptable in society need to know? She needs to appreciate that even when doing nothing, there is a graceful way of doing it; to learn how to stand in a relaxed manner ...

The rules of good deportment are simple, but to carry them out in an effortless manner needs continual concentration ... only then will they become second nature and make one graceful and attractive.

Her problem may be largely solved if through her social club she obtains the opportunity of observing in detail the way in which more sophisticated women behave; how, for example, they apply make-up, enter a room and engage in small talk, and how they select their clothes for particular occasions.[1] For the woman who is already married, the main difficulty is entertaining. Her husband may be wealthy enough to employ male servants, including a cook, but she herself knows nothing about the appropriate ritual. Membership of a dining club, however, enables her to learn this by watching what is done, including the setting of the table, menus, etc. It will provide her with a practical demonstration of the way in which to run an evening party. In addition, the necessity at such formal gatherings of speaking a European language correctly will improve her knowledge of English or French, including socially important expressions and phrases not learned at school. It goes without saying that this greater fluency is valuable for occupational as well as social purposes. For this reason some

[1] Previously, European clothes were *de rigeur* for formal occasions. Nowadays, however, socially prominent women wear frequently an 'African' style of dress, particularly at official parties and receptions. Indicative of this trend—which is largely the result of nationalism—is a recent article in *Nigeria* by Eve de Negri (March 1962) describing the technicalities of style, and design in Yoruba women's fashions.

people join a cultural association, such as the British Council, or take up amateur dramatics. It may be the only opportunity of obtaining continuous practice, because even in educated houses it is customary to use the patois or a native language more often than a European tongue.

Another socially useful skill is dancing, and proficiency is very much admired. Among young people who are educated or have acquired Western tastes in other ways, the preferred style is usually 'ballroom'. In order, therefore, to keep up to date, some associations not only help their members to acquire gramophones of the same size and make, but teach them the latest version of jazz and jive as well as high-life. Each male performer has his female partner to demonstrate steps for the rest of the group. The more traditionally based societies are doubtless popular for analogous reasons. The dancing *compins*, for example, are continuously experimenting with new kinds of dance and rhythm and the best known companies are noted for having introduced certain tunes. Since many such performances are given in public the expert dancers concerned earn applause and may become quite famous.

Finally, voluntary associations assist mobility in several concrete ways. They use their influence to find people better jobs, they facilitate business contacts, and they further a person's professional career.[1] Also, in some cases, they are the means whereby public recognition is given to deserving members of the community at large. This is done by conferring honorific titles, such as Chief, Chief Patron, etc., in widely known organizations like the Reformed Ogboni Society and

[1] In some cases, associations have also helped a person to become rich by less scrupulous means—by charging initiates exorbitant fees for their training. For example, groups of individuals have been known to sponsor a Tigari priest and in return share in the income when he begins his practice (Christensen, p. 277).

Nanemei Akpee.[1] Since the significance of these awards is not confined to the associations' own members they single the recipients out as persons of special distinction. To be honoured in this way—to be known as 'Chief So-and-So'—frequently marks a step upward for a commoner, even a professional man. Also, since it identifies the individual concerned with his ethnic group, it may be very helpful to an aspiring politician seeking traditionally minded supporters.[2]

It is, in fact, the latter considerations which may have the greatest significance for the emerging social structure. It has been shown in general terms that the more 'Western' or the more 'Islamic' an institution the greater its prestige and that the associations with the strictest rules are the most highly regarded. In other words, membership of the societies concerned apparently involves a species of social grading. If, in addition, the reason for joining is that the individual hopes thereby either to gain or to equip himself for a higher status, this implies the existence of class feeling, however unconscious the motivation.

[1] Title-taking in more indigenous associations, such as age-grades, is facilitated by the practice of putting money aside in contribution clubs (Ardener, 1953, p. 141).

[2] Cf. Busia (1956): '. . . the new élite that now has effective political authority, wish not only to make sure of this by eliminating rivals, but also aspire to be a standard-setting group in the traditional and cultural sphere also. Since elected local councillors, and even cabinet ministers, have attempted in different ways, such as being carried in a chief's hammock, or using a chief's staff of office, or wearing chiefly attire, to arrogate to themselves the appurtenances of chieftaincy and of the traditional élite' (pp. 429-30).

CONCLUSION

IN the foregoing analysis the function of voluntary associations has been examined in two ways. Modern West African society exemplified the process of change, and the attempt was made to show the part that they play in adapting traditional institutions and in integrating the new social system. The final task is briefly to consider the wider implications of the propositions offered.

The postulation with which we started is that urbanization is at the heart of social change, giving rise to a new and larger variety of institutions. This proliferation occurs because the industrial forces which provide the main impetus to urban growth largely determine at the same time the pattern of the social system. There is specialization not only of economic activities, but of all the principal activities of community life, including the care and training of children, religion, leisure, law and government. However, owing to the rapidity of technological and other changes, those fresh groupings and institutions—mines, factories, schools, hospitals, churches and municipal councils—tend to develop on their own. Their *raison d'être* is alien to traditional culture and their personnel is recruited according to entirely different principles from kinship and the other factors which people brought up tribally customarily use as criteria. The result, since their functional relation to the older system is weak, is the need, structurally speaking, for an organizational basis upon which integration can proceed.[1]

[1] Using the concept of 'replicate social structure' Robert J. Anderson and Gallatin Anderson have approached comparable problems of social change in modern society in a similar way. They write '. . . the concept of replicate social structure draws attention to a significant structural basis for associational proliferation in recent social change. These formal organizations bridge the

Voluntary associations are important for this general process because, so far as can be judged, they are popular enough[1] to ensure the necessary recruitment in terms of functioning groups. Though relevant statistics are sparse, not only is the proportion of individuals in the cities who belong apparently high, but such information as is available suggests that the average individual is a member of several groups. For example, Mercier has estimated that more than two-thirds of the population of Dakar, women as well as men, belonged to a political party, not to speak of other organizations (1956, pp. 441-52). In two separate samples of householders in Lagos, Marris found that respectively 67 per cent and 51 per cent belonged to societies (p. 137). These facts, coupled with the wide range of membership in terms of age, sex, tribe, religion, occupation, and social class, means that the corresponding network of social ties created on the basis of voluntary associations must be extensive. Interaction is increased further by the marked tendency of particular types of associations—ethnic unions associations, youth groups—to affiliate and to ramify into large organizations on their own. A person may belong at one and the same time to a friendly society, a tribal association, and a recreational group. Even if the membership of these individual groups partly overlaps, it still means that any given person is likely to be brought associationally in contact with a large number of other individuals. The effect of this kind of social field has been described by Barnes as follows:

Each person is, as it were, in touch with a number of other people some of whom are directly in touch with each other and some of

gap between the undefined groupings and the various units of a modern political or business structure. They bureaucratize local institutions. By forming associations, the members of a local group organize themselves so that they can readily articulate with the political or business structure.' (*Southwestern Journal of Anthropology*, Vol. 18, No. 4, 1962, p. 369.)

[1] Lombard, for instance, speaks about 'African societomania' in this regard.

whom are not. Similarly each person has a number of friends, and these friends have their own friends; some of any one person's friends know each other, others do not . . . [1954, p. 43]

In this way an organizational basis is provided for social action in general. However, the significance of the associational network is that it involves not only a large number of individual relationships but the relationship of groups with differing interests and roles. Farmers, traders, clerks, tribal leaders, housewives, politicians, professional men, may all be members of the same association. Their differing interests are expressed in the multiplicity of aims and purposes explicitly or implicitly served by many such associations, which may be concerned at one and the same time with mutual aid, a political cause, recreations, and the maintenance of tribal values. This differentiation of the association's own function may divide the administration into separate compartments, placing individual members in charge of particular activities. Thus, as already explained, the women members are generally organized apart from the men, and in the larger associations it is usual for the officials appointed to have specific duties. In addition to the women's leader, one of them may be responsible for recreation and entertainment, another may supervise the collection of dues and the distribution of benefit, and another act as liaison between the association and a political group.

The significance of this multiplicity of aims and specialization of function is twofold. It means that the individual is prepared for roles he can perform in the urban structure and this assists the growth of new institutions. Since, as a rule, he retains membership of an association it also facilitates integration. The effect has been shown in instances previously quoted—in, for example, the assumption by associational officials of positions of political leadership and the formation of political parties around a nucleus of associations. The latter development gave expression simultaneously to two sets of interests—the modernist ambitions of the young men as a group and the nationalist aspirations of people concerned with African self-government. In other cases, representatives of associations have served along with tribal elders on local government councils and on other official bodies.

The fact that the old and the new institutions are articulated in this way with one another and with bureaucracy draws attention again to inter-relations of adaptation and integration in the process. True, the notion of societies advancing through similar progressive stages no longer is profitable, but what the present data suggest—the disappearance of simple narrow systems of integration in favour of more complex wider systems—is another matter. We need a satisfactory tool for purposes of analysis, and I have tried to show that in the adaptive and integrative function of voluntary associations we have one such model. We may have in this heuristic device a method of tracing the implications of general changes for the definition of particular roles and of showing how the inter-relation of roles influences the course of that change.

REFERENCES CITED

ACHEBE, CHINUA (1960). *No Longer at Ease*. London.

ACQUAH, IONE (1958). *Accra Survey*. London.

ALOBA, ABIODUN (1954). 'Tribal unions in party politics', *West Africa*, vol. XXXVIII, No. 1950.

ARDENER, SHIRLEY G. (1953). 'The social and economic significance of the Contribution Club among a section of the Southern Ibo', *Proceedings, Annual Conference, West African Institute of Social and Economic Research*. Ibadan.

—(n.d.). *The Comparative Study of Rotating Credit Associations*. Unpublished MS.

BAETA, C. G. (1962). *Prophetism in Ghana*. London.

BAKER, TANYA (n.d.). *Women's Elites in Western Nigeria*. Unpublished MS. Department of Social Anthropology, Edinburgh University.

BAKER, TANYA, and BIRD, MARY (1959). 'Urbanization and the position of women', *Sociological Review*, vol. 7, No. 1.

BALANDIER, GEORGES (1953). 'Messianismes et nationalismes en Afrique noire', *Cahiers Internationaux de Sociologie*, vol. XIV.

— (1955a). 'Social changes and problems in Negro Africa', In *Africa in the Modern World*, ed. Stillman, Calvin W. Chicago.

— (1955b). *Sociologie des Brazzavilles Noires*. Paris.

— (1956). 'Urbanism in West and Central Africa', In *Social Implications of Industrialization and Urbanization in Africa South of the Sahara*. Unesco, Paris.

BANDOH, A. A. (n.d.). Unpublished MS.

BANTON, MICHAEL (1957). *West African City: a study of tribal life in Freetown*. London.

BARNES, J. A. (1954). 'Class and Committees in a Norwegian island Parish', *Human Relations*, vol. 7.

BASCOM, WILLIAM (1952). 'The Esusu: a credit institution of the Yoruba', *Journal of the Royal Anthropological Institute*, vol. LXXXII.

— (1955). 'Urbanization among the Yoruba', *American Journal of Sociology*, vol. LX, No. 5.

BAUER, PETER (1954). *West African Trade*. Cambridge.

BIRD, MARY (n.d.). *Social Change and Kinship and Marriage among the Yoruba of Western Nigeria*. Ph.D. Dissertation, Edinburgh University.

BIRD, MARY and BAKER, TANYA (1959). 'Urbanization and the position of women', *Sociological Review*, vol. 7, No. 1.

BUSIA, K. A. (1950). *Social Survey of Sekondi-Takoradi*. Accra.

— (1951). *The Position of the Chief in the Modern Political System of Ashanti*. London.

— (1956). 'The present situation and aspirations of elites in the Gold Coast', *International Social Science Bulletin*, vol. VIII, No. 3.

— (1957). 'Africa in transition', *Project Papers No. 10, World Council of Churches*.

BUTCHER, D. (1954). *The Role of the Fulbe in the Urban Life and Economy of Lunsar, Sierra Leone*. Unpublished Ph.D. thesis, Department of Social Anthropology, Edinburgh University.

CAPRASSE, P. (1959). 'Leaders africains en milieu urbain', *Centre d'Études des Problémes Sociaux Indigènes, Collection de mémoires*, vol. 5.

CAREY, A. T. (n.d.). Unpublished study of Keta, Gold Coast. Department of Social Anthropology, Edinburgh University.

CHRISTENSEN, JAMES BOYD (1962). 'The adaptive functions of Fanti priesthood', In *Continuity and Change in African Cultures*, eds. Bascom, W. R., and Herskovits, M. J. Chicago.

CLARKSON, M. L. (1954). *Report on Enquiry with Regard to Friendly and Mutual Benefit Groups in the Gold Coast*. Accra.

CLÉMENT, PIERRE (1956). 'Social effects of urbanization in Stanleyville, Belgian Congo', In *Social Implications of Industrialization and Urbanization in Africa South of the Sahara*. Unesco, Paris.

COLEMAN, J. S. (1952). 'The role of tribal associations in Nigeria', *Proceedings, Annual Conference, West African Institute of Social and Economic Research*. Ibadan.

— (1958). *Nigeria: Background to Nationalism*. London, Berkeley and Los Angeles.

COMHAIRE, JEAN (1955). 'Sociétés secrètes et mouvements prophétiques au Congo Belge', *Africa*, vol. XXV, No. 1.

COMHAIRE-SYLVAIN, SUZANNE (1950a). 'Food and leisure among the African youth of Leopoldville', *Communications from the Cape Town University School of African Studies*, n.s., No. 25.

— (1950b). 'Associations on the basis of origin in Lagos, Nigeria', *American Catholic Sociological Review*, vol. 11.

— (1951). 'Le travail des femmes à Lagos, Nigeria', *Zaire*, vol. 5, Nos. 2 and 5.

COWAN, L. GRAY (1958). *West African Local Government*. New York.

DESCH, J. (1950). 'Villes d'Afrique occidentale', *Cahiers d'Outre-Mer*, July–September.

DOUCHY, A. and FELDHEIM, P. (1956). Some effects of industrialization in Equatoria Province', In *Social Implications of Industrialization and Urbanization in Africa South of the Sahara*. Unesco, Paris.

EKWENSI, CYPRIAN (1954). *People of the City*. London.

— (1961). *Jagua Nana*. London.

FIAWOO, D. K. (1959a). 'Urbanization and religion in Eastern Ghana', *Sociological Review*, vol. 7, No. 1.

— (1959b). *The Influence of Contemporary Social Changes on the Magico-religious Concepts and Organisation of the Southern Ewe-speaking People of Ghana*. Ph.D. Dissertation, Edinburgh University.

— (1961). *Social Survey of Tefle*. Institute of Education, Child Development Monographs, No. 2. Legon, Ghana.

FIELD, M. J. (1948). *Akim Kotuku, a Gold Coast Native State*. Accra.

FIRTH, RAYMOND (1947). 'Social problems and research in British West Africa', *Africa*, vol. XVII, Nos. 2 and 3.

FORTES, MEYER (1947). 'Ashanti survey, 1945–46: an experiment in social research', *Geographical Journal*, vol. CX.

GAMBLE, DAVID P. (n.d.). Unpublished study of the social structure of Lunsar, Sierra Leone. Department of Social Anthropology, Edinburgh University.

GARIGUE, PHILIP (1953). 'The West African Students' Union', *Africa*, vol. XXIII, No. 1.

GEERTZ, C. 1962 'The Rotating Credit Association: A "Middle Rung" in Development', *Economic Development and Cultural Change*, vol. 10, No. 3.

GLUCKMAN, MAX (1960). 'Tribalism in modern British Central Africa, *Cahiers D'Études Africaines*, No. 1.

GOLD COAST, STATISTICAL DEPARTMENT (1956a). 'Sekondi-Takoradi survey of population and household budgets', *Gold Coast Statistical and Economic Papers*. Accra.

— (1956b). 'Kumasi survey of population and household budgets', *Gold Coast Statistical and Economic Papers*. Accra.

GUILBOT, J. (1947). 'Petite étude sur la main d'œuvre à Douala', *Institut Français d'Afrique Noire, Mémoires*, No. 1.

HAIR, P. E. H. (1953). 'An industrial and urban community in East Nigeria, 1914-1953', *Proceedings, Annual Conference, West African Institute of Social and Economic Research*. Ibadan.

HARRISON-CHURCH, R. J. (1963). *West Africa: A Study of the Environment and of Man's Use of It* (3rd edn). London.

HELLMAN, ELLEN (1937). 'The native in the towns', In *The Bantu-speaking Tribes of South Africa*, ed. Schapera, I. London.

HERSKOVITS, MELVILLE J. (1962). *The Human Factor in Changing Africa*. New York.

HODGKIN, THOMAS (1956). *Nationalism in Colonial Africa*. London.

— (1961). *African Political Parties*. London.

HOLAS, B. (1953). 'La Goumbé', An association of Muslim youth in the lower Ivory Coast, *Kongo-Overzee*, vol. 19.

— (1954). 'Bref aperçu sur les principaux cultes syncrétiques de la basse Côte d'Ivoire', *Africa*, vol. XXIV, No. 1.

JAHODA, GUSTAV (1955). 'The social background of a West African student population', I and II, *British Journal of Sociology*, vol. V, No. 4 and vol. VI, No. 1.

JELLICOE, MARGUERITE R. (1955). 'Women's groups in Sierra Leone, *African Women* (London University, Institute of Education), vol. I, No. 2.

LEITH-ROSS, S. (1956). 'The rise of a new élite among the women of Nigeria', *International Social Science Bulletin*, vol. VIII, No. 3.

LITTLE, KENNETH L. (1951). *The Mende of Sierra Leone*. London.

— (1955a). 'The African élite in British West Africa', in *Race Relations in World Perspective*, ed. Lind, A. Honolulu.

— (1955b). 'Structural change in the Sierra Leone Protectorate', *Africa*, vol. XXV, No. 3.

— (1957). 'The role of voluntary associations in West African urbanization', *American Anthropologist*, vol. 59, No. 4.

— (1959a). 'The organisation of voluntary associations in West Africa', *Civilisations*, vol. IX, No. 3.

— (1959b). Introduction, 'Urbanism in West Africa', *Sociological Review*, vol. 7, No. 1.

LITTLEJOHN, JAMES (n.d.). Unpublished pilot study of Lunsar, Sierra Leone. Department of Social Anthropology, Edinburgh University.

LLOYD, PETER C. (1953). 'Craft organizations in Yoruba towns', *Africa*, vol. XXIII, No. 1.

— (1959). 'The Yoruba town today', *Sociological Review*, vol. 7, No. 1.

LOMBARD, J. (1954). 'Cotonou: ville africaine', *Bulletin de l'Institut Français d'Afrique Noire*, vol. XVI(B), Nos. 3 and 4.

McCall, D. F. (1961). 'Trade and the role of wife in a modern West African town', in *Social Change in Modern Africa*, ed. Southall, A. W. London.

Marshall, Gloria A. (1962). The Marketing of Farm Produce: Some Patterns of Trade Among Women in Western Nigeria, *Nigerian Institute of Social and Economic Research. Conference Proceedings*. Ibadan.

Marris, Peter (1961). *Family and Social Change in An African City*. London.

Martin, E. C. (1923). 'Early educational experiments on the Gold Coast', *Journal of the African Society*, vol. 23.

Mercier, Paul (1954). 'Aspects des problèmes de stratification sociale dans l'Ouest africain', *Cahiers Internationaux de Sociologie*, vol. XVII.

— (1956a). 'An experimental investigation into occupational and social categories in Dakar', in *Social Implications of Industrialization and Urbanization in Africa South of the Sahara*. Unesco, Paris.

— (1956b). 'Evolution of Senegalese élites', *International Social Science Bulletin*, vol. VIII, No. 3.

Messenger, John C. (1959). 'Religious acculturation among the Anang Ibibio', in *Continuity and Change in African Cultures*, eds. Bascom, W. R. and Herskovits, M. J. Chicago.

Morton-Williams, Peter (1953). 'Social consequences of industrialisation among the South Western Yoruba', *Proceedings, Annual Conference, West African Institute of Social and Economic Research*. Ibadan.

Nadel, S. F. (1942). *A Black Byzantium*. London.

Nigeria, Department of Statistics (1950). *Population Census of Lagos, 1950*. Lagos.

— (1953). *Population Census of the Eastern Region of Nigeria*. Lagos.

Offodile, E. P. Oyeaka (1947). 'Growth and influence of tribal unions', *West African Review*, vol. XVIII, No. 239.

Ottenberg, Phoebe V. (1959). 'The changing economic position of women among the Afikpo Ibo', in *Continuity and Change in African Cultures*, eds. Bascom, W. R. and Herskovits, M. J. Chicago.

Ottenberg, S. (1955). 'Improvement associations among the Afikpo Ibo', *Africa*, vol. XXV, No. 1.

Parrinder, Geoffrey (1953). *Religion in an African City*. London.

Pauvert, J. C. (1955). 'La problème des classes sociales dans l'Afrique équatoriale', *Cahiers Internationaux de Sociologie*, vol. XIX.

REFERENCES

PORTER, ARTHUR T. (1953). 'Religious affiliation in Freetown, Sierra Leone', *Africa*, vol. XXIII, No. 1.

— (1963). *Creoledom*. London.

PROTHERO, R. M. (1958). *Migrant Labour from Sokoto Province, Northern Nigeria*. Government Printer, Northern Nigeria.

ROUCH, JEAN (1954). *Migration in the Gold Coast* (English translation). Accra.

ROUCH, JEAN and BERNUS, E. (1959). 'Notes sur les prostitués 'toutou' de Treichville et d'Adjamé', *Études eburnéenes*, vol. VI.

RUEL, M. J. (1954). 'The Modern Adaptation of Associations among the Banyang of the West Cameroons', *Southwestern Journal of Anthropology*, vol. 20, No. 1.

SMITH, J. NOEL (1963). *The Presbyterian Church of Ghana, 1835–1960; a younger church in a changing society*. Ph.D. Dissertation, Edinburgh University.

SMITH, MARY F. (1955). *Baba of Karo, a Woman of the Muslim Hausa*. New York.

SMITH, M. G. (1957). 'Co-operation in Hausa society', *Information*, vol. X.

SMYTHE, HUGH H. and MABEL M. (1960). *The New Nigerian Elite*. Stanford.

SOUTHALL, AIDAN W. (1961). 'Population movements in East Africa', in *Essays on African Population*, eds. Barbour, K. M. and Prothero, R.M. London.

TARDITS, C. (1958). *Porto Novo*. Paris.

UNITED NATIONS ECONOMIC COMMISSION FOR AFRICA (1962). Introduction to the Problems of Urbanization in Tropical Africa, Part I. *Workshop on Urbanization in Africa*. Addis Ababa.

WALLERSTEIN, IMMANUEL (1960). 'Ethnicity and national integration in West Africa', *Cahiers d'Études Africaines*, No. 3.

— (1963). 'The political role of voluntary associations in Middle Africa', in *Political Groups in Middle Africa*, eds. Coleman, J. S. and Rosberg, Carl. Also in *Urbanization in African Social Change*. Centre of African Studies, Edinburgh University.

WARD, BARBARA E. (1956). 'Some observations on religious cults in Ashanti', *Africa*, vol. XXVI, No. 1.

WARMINGTON, W. A., ARDENER, EDWIN, and ARDENER, SHIRLEY (1960). *Plantation and Village in the Cameroons*. London.

INDEX

Abeokuta, 118, 127

Abidjan, 18, 44, 63, 133, 155n

Accra, 15, 16, 17, 18, 19, 21, 22, 25, 27, 28, 30n, 33, 47n, 48, 66n, 68, 69, 72, 77, 79, 81, 82, 86, 91, 124, 128n, 133n, 145, 155n;
Accra Turf Club, 82

Achebe, Chinua, 29n, 32n, 98, 141n

Achimota, Old Boys' Association, 76

Action Group (Nigeria), 147

Adangme, the, 47n

Advanced Babua Women's Association, 75

Akan, 73

Aku, the, 157

Akwamu, the, 30n

Alikali Societies, 130n

Alimony, 122

Alliance Francaise, 77

Ambas Geda, 105-6

Americans, 151

Anang, the, 37n, 94

Anglican Church, 70

Anlo, 28, 38, 41-2

Apostolic Revelation Society, 69

Apprenticeship, 58-9, 90

Arbitration, 95

Ashanti, 9, 14, 16, 32, 68

Asians, 128

Aso-ebi, 64

Associations, Voluntary, *see* Voluntary Associations; *and for specific types, see* 'Cultural', Political, Tribal *and* Women's Associations; Dining, Social *and* Sports Clubs; Recreational Companies; Syncretist Cults; Benefit *and* 'Christian' Societies

Atike movement, 37

Atwima Society, 32-3

Azikiwe, Nnamdi, 77, 107, 108

Bamako, 76

Bambara, the, 37, 155n

Bank, National, 34

Baptism, 44, 45

Baptists, 70

Bar, the, 139
Bar Association, 154

Bars, 11, 77, 131

'Been-to', 141

Benefit Societies, 28, 48, 145, 155; Ibo, 52-4; Moslem, 55; women's, 56; Yoruba, 52; social activities, 54;
Bo United Moslem Women's, 56
Nanemei Akpee, 48-51, 125, 162
Yehowa Kpee, 54-5
See also Contribution Clubs *and* Mutual Aid

Benefits, Financial, 65, 67, 73, 128;
Commercial, 35, 125
Educational, 28, 33-4, 76, 80
Family, 48
Funeral, 28, 32, 33, 56, 57, 68, 73, 132
Loans, 35, 48, 49, 53n
Matrimonial, 33
Medical and Sickness, 48, 49, 57, 68, 69
Officiary, 33

Bequests, Charitable, 74

Bibiani, 28

Bible classes, 67

Blekete, 37-42, 94

Bo, 18, 129;
African Club, 77-9
School, 75
United Moslem Women's Society, 56

Bogosu, 28

Boxing, 73, 82

'Boys London', 106

Brazzaville, 63, 132

British Council, 77, 161

Busanga, the, 15n

Calabar, 28
Calabaris, 129

173